The Nature of Mental Things

ARTHUR W. COLLINS

UNIVERSITY OF NOTRE DAME PRESS
NOTRE DAME, INDIANA

Library of Congress Cataloging-in-Publication Data

Collins, Arthur W.
  The nature of mental things.

  Includes index.
  1. Thought and thinking.   2. Belief and doubt.
3. Consciousness.   4. Teleology.   I. Title.
B105.T54C65   1986   128'.2   86-40242
ISBN 0-268-01463-9

Manufactured in the United States of America

FOR LINDA

THE NATURE OF MENTAL THINGS

Contents

Preface

As an undergraduate I studied some mathematics, and, like many, I particularly admired the aesthetic character of abstract algebra and projective geometry in algebraic presentation. In trying to understand and to construct proofs for propositions in these fields I found myself informally adopting a kind of imagery with the help of which it seemed easier to think about these subjects. The images were themselves rather abstract or sketchy, and they varied somewhat for different problems and contexts. The images might be just arrays of things like little pegs connected by threads to represent mappings and so on. This was not an attempt to create a model or to achieve detailed representation of the conceptual structures at stake. It just seemed to help to have something in mind to which to refer very abstract ideas, even though the pictures formed for the purpose did not try to do justice to the logical complexities they represented for me in a general way. I did not think, of course, that the mathematical propositions in which I was interested were really descriptions of the things I imagined. The help that imagined objects gave me did not make me think that, in the absence of something or other in the rôle of my pictures, the mathematical propositions could not be true. The images functioned in an innocent heuristic way without encouraging any ontological extravagance. I suppose that most or even all people thinking about such matters create private pictures in this way to help handle abstract objects and their complex interrelations.

Something like this constructive imagining takes place in the thinking of philosophers of mind. Our conception of our own mental lives, when we enter on philosophical speculation, seems to be facilitated by imagining a subject matter composed of inner entities, states, and relationships to which we refer propositions about beliefs, memories, intentions, desires, and perceptual experiences. These imagined realities, however, are not so innocent of ontological implications. They are easily promoted to the status of the real subject of our discourse when we speak of "mental phenomena." At worst, we philosophers

tend to think, the imagined entities, states, and relationships are provisional conceptions. Our characterization of mental things may need
a lot of refinement before we attain a correct picture of them, we say
to ourselves. But, unlike the mathematical case, we certainly do suppose that if there were not anything in the rôle of these realities, our
assertions about mental phenomena would not be true at all.

For example, the things that a person learns and has not forgot-
ten are said to be beliefs that are "retained" in the believer's mind.
We readily imagine retained beliefs as stored entities like the several
contents of files where old records are kept. All the things that a person can remember are in this storage, and when he can no longer
remember something, that is because the stored item has faded,
disintegrated, or been discarded. Since we represent a person's beliefs
via the sentences that he might use in order to express things he believes
and that we might use in asking him about his beliefs, the stored beliefs
are easily pictured as something like a list of sentences in a person.
In philosophy, I say, these imaginative aids do not function as innocent heuristic devices to which we attach no literal significance. On
the contrary, we are very much tempted to think that the constituents
of our mental lives must be realities like the things we imagine, and
a number of contemporary philosophers have gone so far as to propose stored inscriptions of sentences as the actual form in which a person's beliefs are retained in him.

Just a little bit of reflection makes this idea seem implausible.
For each of the things a subject believes there are a very large number
of different sentences, any one of which he would recognize as suitable
for the expression of that particular belief. Indefinitely large sets of
such sentences are generated by syntactical and semantical transformations which leave their assertive content unchanged. Are all these
sentences stored in the believer? Or is just one of them stored? Or
a few? Furthermore, endless sentences express different contents that
are trivially generated from one belief, and they will have to be regarded
as formulations of further beliefs of a subject. Thus, if S believes that
the sun is 93 million miles from the earth, then of course S believes
the sun is more than 92 million miles from the earth, and more than
one mile, and more than 105 and 7/8ths inches, and so on without
end. All of these sentences have different contents, and they all express things that S surely believes.

These very simple reflections ought to be enough to incline us to set aside not only the idea of storage of beliefs in sentential form but the idea of inner storage of beliefs altogether. If beliefs were items stored in a believer, sentential inscriptions would be a good form for storage from a conceptual point of view. The counterintuitive consequences of the idea of inner storage for each belief are merely brought into a clear light by the inner-inscription picture. The implausibility will still be there, although we drop the inner sentences. The problem brought to light is the fact that we actually have no conception of beliefs which would enable us to answer the question "Just what is to count as one stored belief?" We really do not know what we are talking about when we say that a belief is an inner reality of some kind.

When we think of a subject's beliefs, we will not readily get rid of the idea of associating them with sentences. We will always say that S believes that p and q, but he does not believe that r, and that he is undecided on s. There is nothing whatever wrong with this way of speaking. On the contrary, it is plainly indispensable for thought and discourse about belief. Thinking of the things that a person believes in terms of the sentences that might be used to express those beliefs is innocuous, as long as we do not think that the use of sentences here is a commitment to the view that beliefs are realities in believers that are, if not actually inscriptions of sentences in some language or code, then inner representations of some other sort, or in any case inner states or processes of some kind or other.

In the present climate of thinking, however, philosophers of mind are ever ready to construe the devices of our discourse and thought about beliefs as if they were references to inner realities about which our statements are claims. The familiarity of problems facing inner inscriptions as the vehicle for the storage of beliefs do not inhibit this readiness to take the language of stored information literally. Even storage in sentential form is not abandoned. Philosophers seem to hope that the "problems" generated by the idea of inner inscriptions will get solved when we have more scientific knowledge of neural functioning. The concept of inner realities has so powerful a grip on our imagination here that it is little affected by serious and, perhaps, even absolutely insurmountable obstacles.

Wittgenstein once said that philosophers are like savages who place a false interpretation on the discourse of civilized men and then draw outlandish conclusions. Are philosophical conceptions of mental life as constituted of inner realities an illustration of such philosophical barbarism? That would mean that ordinary men, as contrasted with philosophers, do not construe their discourse about beliefs as claims about inner realities in people.

Suppose a subject finds out something about the world. For example, he learns that Cicero denounced Cataline. Then he might tell another, "Cicero denounced Cataline." He would speak, of course, not of anything in himself but of the affairs of some long-dead Romans. It is just this bit of history of which he is apprized and on which he "reports." If he is unsure, afraid that it might, perhaps, have been Cataline that denounced Cicero, he could say, "I believe that Cicero denounced Cataline." And accepting his statement, we will understand that he has this belief and report of him, "He believes that Cicero denounced Cataline." Is not this a good example of the way discourse about belief gets its footing among ordinary speakers for ordinary purposes? A speaker will say, "I believe that p," rather than asserting merely p because he recognizes an appreciable chance that he is wrong. This does not substitute an inner reality on which he reports for the outer-world subject matter of p. It is just an outer matter that he makes a claim about and about which he may be wrong. He uses the sentence in expressing a belief, and we use it in ascribing belief to him, not because there is a something like a sentence, or some other form of representation present within him, but merely to put into words what it is about the world that he apprehends, or is mistaken about. The words "Cicero denounced Cataline" in their occurrence in S's expression of belief or in our ascription of belief do themselves constitute a representation. They serve to represent the denunciation of Cataline by Cicero and do not report another behind-the-scenes representation in the believer. Nothing inner has come into play, but discourse about belief does come into play. Perhaps "civilized" men make no assumption that statements about beliefs assert that something is present in the believer.

But the belief is retained. A day or ten years later the subject can still tell us, "Cicero denounced Cataline, or, anyway, I believe he did." Was not the belief stored? If it was not stored, would not the later expression of this belief be a miracle? This question is characteristic of the pressure to which philosophers succumb without much resistance. If he still has the belief, he must have kept it, somehow, in the interval. So we say that beliefs ought to be things that can be stored in people. But, in fact, how S manages to remember that Cicero denounced Cataline is one question, and whether beliefs are inner items in believers is quite another.

Maybe S has a bad memory which he reinforces by writing down what he learns in a notebook and reviewing the notebook before saying what he has learned of history. Then he stores what he has learned in sentence-form in a notebook, and that explains S's later ability to produce the information. But when he says, "Cicero denounced Cataline, or, anyway, I believe he did," he is not speaking of his notebook, and his belief is not literally stored in it. A person could make claims about his notebook, and he could have beliefs about and knowledge about his notebook, as well as beliefs and knowledge about Roman history. So he might tell us, "Here in my notebook, in my own handwriting, I find 'Cicero denounced Cataline'." But he will not thus express the belief that Cicero did denounce Cataline. We could plausibly ask him, "And do you suppose what you wrote there is true? Do you believe that Cicero denounced Cataline?" The answer could be either Yes or No.

If we all kept detailed notebooks, we might fall into a habit of speech according to which we called the entries in a person's notebook his "beliefs," and we might look into another's notebook in order to find out what he believes on some point without troubling him to answer questions. "He thinks Cicero denounced Cataline" we might report on finding "Cicero denounced Cataline" in S's notebook. But we will not be tempted to erect a real identity theory on this usage. We will know that this convenient way of speaking rests on the assumption that when S wrote this, he did so because he believed it, and when S looks at his notebook himself, he will be reminded or, in any case, he will take it that what is written therein is true. So S will be willing to say, "Cicero denounced Cataline." Or he will say, "I believe that Cicero denounced Cataline." The latter formulation includes an element of guardedness because S is not sure that the denunciation was made, but it remains a tentative claim about Roman history and is not a report on what it says in the notebook. If he were merely to report the sentential inscription, he would not express a belief about Roman history at all, although he would express a true belief about his notebook.

Even if S always relies on his notebook, so that we need never ask him whether he believes what is written in it, we and S and everyone else will know that S's belief is not constituted of an inscription in a notebook. And this is not simply because the notebook is a physical object external to S and a part of the world he has to experience and interpret. It is because to believe that Cicero denounced Cataline one must stand to be right or wrong depending on whether Cicero denounced Cataline or not. S will only be right or wrong on that issue if, in addition to storing the inscription in the notebook, and retrieving it as occasion requires, he takes it to be a true inscription.

The conceptual rôle that might be played by stored neural inscriptions or inner mental representations of any other kind will be the same rôle as that played here by sentences written in a notebook. We cannot reasonably claim that it is really impossible that anything like inscriptions should be stored in a brain, or impossible that stored inscriptions might be retrieved by some neural mechanism, nor can we deny a priori that such inner representations and their retrieval might play a rôle in our ability to remember things. Let us suppose all this is discovered to be true one day by a team of neurologists and information theorists. That will be a banner day for the materialist philosophy of mind! Without any doubt from then on we would adopt a way of speaking in which we call the inner representations "beliefs" of the person in whose brain we find them, just as we could call the inscriptions in a notebook the owner's beliefs. But the neurophysiological discovery and this natural way of speaking will give us no reason at all for thinking that the subject's beliefs have now been identified and that to believe that Cicero denounced Cataline *is* to have the appropriate representation in one's brain.

On the hypothesis that this discovery is made, we will have found that a mechanism like keeping notes in a notebook operates neurally, unconsciously, and automatically, and we will have found a neural mechanism that explains how S is able to state the fact that Cicero denounced Cataline, though he learned it long ago. When such a mechanism is outer, not automatic, and is consciously employed, as a notebook is, we have no trouble appreciating the fact that the naturalness of calling the inscriptions therein "the beliefs" of the owner of the notebook is not a reason for thinking that they really constitute his believing what he does. But this is just what we do think as materialist philosophers of mind when we envision an inner mechanism that might accomplish the same thing. A consultable inscription may function in explaining memory, but it cannot constitute belief. Belief requires supposing that Cicero did denounce Cataline and cannot reduce to having and consulting an inscription to that effect, whether the inscription is outer or inner, and whether the consultation is conscious or unconscious, laborious or automatic.

Wittgenstein discussed the temptation that philosophers feel to explain our capacity to recognize things via the storage of images. How do we manage to follow an order, he asks, such as "Go and pick a red flower"? A proposed philosophical theory has it that in learning to recognize colors we come to be equipped with mental images of them and that once in the field we just find a flower that matches the mental image of red we have in our mind. Wittgenstein pointed out that the logical power of the explanatory theory is no greater because the images are inner and mental. We might as well be equipped with sample color cards, and we might use our cards, finding a flower to match the red card. The emptiness of this "theory" is obvious. When we get to the field and get out our color cards, how do we pick out the red card? If we a need an account here, then the theory has not explained color recognition at all. And if we can simply recognize the color cards and, somehow, need no procedure, then we could use that power on the flowers themselves, so that the cards are superfluous. Inner mental images cannot do any better job of explaining color recognition than outer physical images. Our inclination to think they might illustrates what Wittgenstein called appeal to the mere occultness of the mental.

Theories of inner mental things are frequently subject to this kind of criticism, even though they are not propounded by dualists committed to an occult substance as in Wittgenstein's discussion. The trouble with the theory of inner states of belief is in the logical structure of the account that is supposed to make things intelligible to us. This trouble has nothing to do with the metaphysical category to which we incline to assign such inner items. S can possess representations, and they can somehow be consulted, maybe automatically and unconsciously, in reminding S of who denounced whom. But an outer, consciously retrieved inscription cannot constitute a belief, and the obstacles to such an "identification" are not overcome at all by putting the inscription inside the believer and letting the retrieval and consultation be neural, unconscious, and automatic.

The rise of materialism engendered hopes that the occultness of the mental would be swept aside by the tough-minded outlook of empirical science. Instead of this we find the rhetoric and the prestige of science pressed into service for theoretical speculations that closely follow those of the dualists, and an appeal to the occultness of the mental has been replaced by a very similar appeal to the wonders that will allegedly be revealed by neural science some day.

If I am right and we come to recognize the intrinsic defects of the theories about inner mental things, this will considerably alter our expectations about the course that neural science may be expected to follow. We will not be so confident that there *must be* inner representations like those whose discovery we have just posited for the sake of argument. Perhaps we will always imagine something *as though* it were an inner realm to which discourse about mental concepts makes reference. We may not ever give up this pattern of thinking any more than we will give up the idea that neural fibers are channels through which "information" passes, just as telephone lines are. The message-carrying interpretation of the nervous system is here to stay. We will continue to say that a belief is stored information. Some neural mechanism retrieves it and presents it in the form of an audible utterance when a person remembers what he believes. So the whole process is just like the one exemplified when the electronically stored information in the "memory" of a computer is retrieved and presented in visible form on the screen. This way of thinking makes sense at one level, and it undoubtedly helps in organizing our understandings of both the nervous system and computers. But we cannot take all the metaphors in this style of thinking as if they were not metaphors at all. A nerve fiber is not like a telephone line in that there is no one inside answering the phone. A neural inscription cannot really be a belief any more than a notation on a piece of paper can be a belief. Maybe computers will be built which deserve to be called believers. If so they will have beliefs corresponding to the sentences stored in them if, as believers do, the computers take those sentences to be true. Short of such machines, information is stored in computers only in the sense in which it is also stored in books. The inscriptions in both cases really deserve the title "information" only as a consequence of relations to believers such as ourselves. Beliefs are no more neural realities storable in brains than algebraic groups are arrays of little pegs connected by threads.

The mathematical analogy can be overstated. The imagined physical objects do not capture the "reference" of mathematical concepts because mathematical objects must remain abstract else they will fail to express the ideas for which they are intended. When it comes to mental concepts, we make a mistake in thinking that they really refer to realities of any kind. We can use referring concepts such as the concept of inscriptions of sentences *for convenience* as a way of speaking of a person's beliefs. "All his beliefs about the matter are in this letter he has sent us," we can say. But we must moderate our philosophical savagery and not take this kind of usage literally when we say that his beliefs are stored in his mind, or in his brain.

I develop this line of thought in connection with several different mental concepts. In chapter 1 I sketch the theme of inner realities, in part historically and in part conceptually, and I emphasize the affinity of all the contemporary philosophies of mind with Cartesian antecedents. Chapters 2 and 3 consider the concept of *belief* in detail. Chapter 4 examines our propensity to think of *consciousness* in terms of a range of inner phenomena accessible to the subject. Chapter 5 is ontologically deflationary vis-à-vis the concept of *perceptual experience*, and *visual experience* in particular. Chapter 6 treats the concept of reason-giving explanation. The idea that such explanations, citing beliefs and desires, are causal has played a major part in reinforcing the philosophical contention that beliefs and desires are inner realities. If they can have causal efficacy, then beliefs and desires have to be inner things of the sort that can cause something. This chapter shows that a causal interpretation is not feasible here and explains the teleological structure of reason-giving. Chapter 6 is a slightly altered version of "Action, Causality and Teleological Explanation," *Midwest Studies in Philosophy*, volume IX, University of Minnesota Press, 1984; and it appears here with permission of the publisher. Chapter 7 presents further lines of thought that make it intuitively agreeable that desires and beliefs should not be thought inner realities and connects these themes with the conclusions of chapter 2.

This makes for a radical point of view in the philosophy of mind because all of the contending theories that presently receive any significant backing are variations on the theme of inner mental reality. Taking the long view, it seems to me that this inner-reality conception is really the radical view in the philosophy of mind and that my critical rejection of it is not radical at all, but quite close to common sense. The idea of inner beliefs, desires, experiences, and other "phenomena" of which we are conscious profits in part from our long habituation with a certain expendable orientation in the philosophy of mind. The definitive conception of the mind as a domain of inner realities was radical and innovative in the seventeenth century when it first came to dominate philosophy through the egocentric skeptical perspective of the Cartesian epistemological project. Victims of the same misunderstood paradigms, many philosophers of mind today are still thinking in the same terms.

A considerable danger exists that the mere suggestion that all these ideas of inner mental things should be put aside will sound like madness, as though it were the suggestion that we are not conscious at all, that there are no beliefs, that we have no experiences or desires. That would be a radical view! But no such view is intended. In order to understand what it really means to say that we believe, desire, have experience, are conscious, and so on, nothing will replace a meticulous contemplation of each of these concepts in the setting of its actual use in our affairs. The chapters of the present work are meant in the spirit of such contemplation. At best they are a beginning.

This study tries to rethink the old paradigms and relax the grip of the idea of inner constituents of mental life. Although I find myself in fundamental disagreement with most views now defended, there are many whose writings and thoughts have helped form my own ideas in the philosophy of mind. I am most influenced by Wittgenstein. In important ways G. Ryle, B.A. Farrell, W. Sellars, T. Nagel, D. Dennett, Z. Vendler, and S. Kripke have all been sources of enlightenment for me. It goes without saying that I do not claim that these philosophers agree with what is presented here, and frequently I argue directly against their views. I am also happy to acknowledge my gratitude to my philosophical friends Stanley Eveling, Charles Landesman, and Howard Wettstein for their help and encouragement over many years. If there is value in this work, it owes much to these generous friends. I would also like to thank Joseph Stapleton for his help in the production stages of the book.

Prospects for the Philosophy of Mind

1. Intuitive thoughts about the mental

In spite of waves of behaviorist thinking, and partly because of the failure of behaviorist programs, philosophers of mind are too quick to accept the idea of an inner subject matter comprised of mental states and mental processes. Devoting little preliminary reflection to the ideas that we have of mental phenomena prior to sophisticated analysis, philosophers proceed forthwith to the level of theory construction. Various versions of the mind-brain identity theory and functionalist identity are the theories most discussed at present. These are identity theories in that they take as the fundamental business of the philosophy of mind the identification of the different mental items such as beliefs, desires, and perceptual experiences of which the putative inner subject matter is thought to be composed.

The mind and mental phenomena have always been mysterious and they are a perennial locus of philosophical effort. The long dominance of dualist and idealist philosophies of mind are testimony to the fact that mental phenomena are sufficiently troubling philosophically to encourage extravagant hypotheses and theories. The viewpoint that engendered these extravagances is retained by contemporary theorists who confine their efforts to trying to propose better hypotheses to account for mental phenomena conceived much as the dualists and idealists conceived them. This study is motivated by the conviction that the starting point accepted by most or all of the movements and schools in the philosophy of mind since the Renaissance has to be reconstructed before progress in this field can take place.

Identity theories start by taking it for granted that mental phenomena are processes, states, activities, entities, or properties that go on in, or are found in, or are exemplified in those creatures that

1

have a mental life. This starting point expresses a particular understanding of what is troubling about the mental. Mental phenomena are realities of some kind. The philosopher who tries to *identify* these realities is trying to say *what these rather puzzling phenomena really are.*

In contrast to the starting point of identity theories, I begin from the conviction that our pretheoretical and intuitive ideas about mental phenomena, that is, our ordinary thinking about beliefs, perceptual experiences, desires, sensations, memories, intentions, and other constituents of mental reality ought to be subjected to a critical examination before we can be confident that we have any subject matter here consisting of inner items standing to be identified in some way or other.

Some prephilosophical conceptions of mental things are either ignored by philosophers of mind or treated as if they were principles, and erroneous principles at that, of a rival philosophical theory. It seems to me that, at this level of pretheoretical intuition, we do think that mental things are *private*, and we do think that mental phenomena are *not part of the physical order of things*. In contrast, the view that beliefs, desires, and other mental things are inner states or processes is not an intuitive conviction commonly accepted prior to any philosophical theorizing. I will try to explain this contention about intuitive thinking below. Supposing that these are prevailing intuitive conceptions, they can certainly be mistaken. But if they are our naive ideas, they are part of what we are talking about in the first place, part of what leads us to efforts at sophisticated analysis and theory, and, as such, these naive ideas should not be altogether neglected.

Contemporary philosophers of mind seem to think that it is primarily Cartesian dualists who think that mental things are private and nonphysical. The assumption is that, for bad reasons, or maybe even good reasons,[1] Descartes chose to introduce occult nonmaterial things into his ontology, and Descartes was followed in this error by the whole tradition of classical empiricism. Of course, it is true that Cartesianism exerted a tremendous influence in the development of modern thought, and this is especially a consequence of the adoption of the Cartesian philosophy of mind by the empiricists. But dualist philosophers did not have to invent the idea of privacy and the thought that mental things are not part of the physical world.

Materialist philosophers of mind also think of the dualism they oppose as an earlier theory that, like their own, takes the form of an identity theory. Dualists tried to identify the same inner constituents of mental activity, and from the perspective of modern materialism, the main difference is that dualists do not identify these inner things correctly. In considering this side of the thinking of identity theorists I return repeatedly to the formulations of J.J.C. Smart. Smart thinks in terms of immediately experienced mental phenomena which are ongoing inner events reported by subjects. These inner phenomena constitute the subject matter that is identified by dualists with "goings-on in an immaterial substance" and by materialists with "goings-on inside our skulls."[2]

As an identity theory, dualism is the prototype for modern anti-dualist identity theories, and Smart's "topic-neutral" descriptions are offered by him as characterizations of inner mental things which can be accepted by both dualists and materialists who will differ only over the metaphysical identification of these things.

I would say that materialists are quite right in their conviction that the dualist identity theory is not a good or a successful philosophy of mind and that it is the job of philosophers to try to find a better understanding of the mind and mental things. We have to look to naive thought to see whether or not another philosophy of mind, rightly conceived as a replacement for Cartesian dualism, ought to be just another identity theory which differs from dualism only, or primarily, in proposing a different identity for the very items that dualists identify. The preliminary intuition that mental phenomena are private and not constituents of the physical order, which I have ascribed to pre-philosophical thinking about the mind, does not include the idea that mental concepts are concepts of inner states or inner processes calling for an identification. Identity theory is a format for the philosophy of mind inherited from Cartesian dualism. This Cartesian conception is not opposed or even examined by contemporary materialists or functionalists. It is simply taken over as if it were indisputably correct. The naive view that mental concepts are not concepts of things or events in the physical world may be correct, although the Cartesian thesis that they are concepts of things or events in nonphysical reality is not correct at all.

Furthermore, we have to look to naive thought in order to understand why dualist philosophers were so much as tempted by the views that they put forth, and how those views were able to exert such a decisive influence for so long. This is not just a matter of mistakes generated by some influential philosophical theorists. In examining naive thinking about the mind we shall come to the conclusion that materialist and functionalist identity theories that *now* exert a decisive influence succumb to the very same ill-considered temptations that led Cartesian and empiricist identity theorists astray before them.

2. Privacy

But is it true that pretheoretical intuitions about mental phenomena include the thoughts that they are private and are not part of the physical order of things? Let us consider the claim about privacy first. I want to begin with a disclaimer. As a philosophical doctrine, the thesis that inner mental objects are private *because they are objects of a privileged access via an infallible introspective consciousness* is presently out of favor. That thesis belonged to epistemological enterprises which are now mostly defunct. This is as it should be. I have no desire to rehabilitate any of these *philosophical* conceptions of privacy or the discarded epistemological programs. None of these ideas, so familiar in modern philosophy, are expressions of the naive thought of the privacy of the mental. For all of these theories and claims are based on the view that mental phenomena are inner realities of some kind, realities to which we have this supposed special access. I do not think that the innerness of the mental, presupposed by so many philosophers, is a feature of naive intuitive thought.

Quite independently of any theory or program, most people do know about their own mental states much of the time. They can tell others about them with a certain authority. Maybe there is room for error here, and maybe there are plenty of actual errors. Such errors notwithstanding, the statements people make about their own beliefs, desires, perceptual experiences, intentions, sensations, memories, and the rest of the constituents of their mental lives are usually correct. Furthermore, although people do know about their own mental states and processes, they do not get to know about them *by perceiving* those mental states and processes. They neither see nor hear their beliefs and desires. They *feel* their sensations, but this is not the perceptual "feel" with which we feel the smoothness of silk or the lightswitch in the dark. No philosopher has ever proposed that we do come to know about our own mental states by means of sense perception, so we can simply record the fact that we do not perceive them.

Much of the naive idea of privacy comes from just this fact. We have no naive explanation for our knowledge of our own mental states. (Our situation is hardly better when it comes to sophisticated explanations, but we are not concerned with success or failure at the sophisticated level for the moment.) Whether there is some special means by which we get to know about our own mental states, or whether there is, perhaps, no means at all, is not something on which we have a natural conviction. But we do have a strong conviction that it is only our own mental states and not those of any other person that we do know about, with or without some special way of knowing about them. Of course, we often do know of the mental states of others, but there is no puzzling question concerning how we get to know about their mental states.

The problem of other minds seems to contradict this last assertion. Is it not precisely the puzzling question of how we know the mental states of others? In practice, we learn of others' mental phenomena by conversing with them and by understanding their actions. The problem of other minds is the epistemological problem of the possibility of using these sources, which are conceded to be ordinary and empirical, as a foundation for knowledge of the mental lives of others. The point is that if we have knowledge of the mental phenomena of others we acquire it by ordinary means much as we acquire information about the physical world. This is not how we come to know the presence and character of our own mental phenomena. The existence of the problem of other minds actually registers the distinction to which I am calling attention.

Therefore, when we note that it is absurd to suppose that perception gives me knowledge of my desire for a raise in pay, or that I perceive my belief that interest rates will fall, it is taken for granted that we are talking only about *my* apprehension of *my* desires and *my* beliefs. If I do know about your desires and beliefs, I do not perceive them either, but there has to be some ordinary way in which I get to know about them such as your telling me or my inferring your mental state from your behavior, which I do perceive. I certainly do not get at your mental states in the way, or lack of a way, in which I get at my own. This can sound like an invocation of privileged access, but it is not. I have no view about what sort of access I have to my mental states, and I do not even know whether there is room for the notion of access to something when it comes to my mental states. But I do know that I believe that p, and that I desire x.

It seems that the idea of the privacy of the mental does precede theory. Long before we philosophize we all appreciate not only that it is possible and often easy to conceal one's thoughts and feelings, and to keep one's memories and desires to oneself, but also we appreciate that if our mental activities are to be known by others at all, it is commonly necessary for us to make a point of communicating them. We may decide to repudiate the philosophical doctrines based on introspection or any kind of privileged access. We cannot fail to notice that each person naturally knows and can talk effortlessly about the constituents of his own mental life as he does not know and cannot talk effortlessly about the mental life of anyone else. This is immediately connected with the fact that we do not perceive our mental states. Each person is acquainted with his own birthmarks and warts. But he perceives these just as others do, and it is therefore conceded that another's familiarity with these things is of the same sort and could equal or surpass one's own. Mental things stand in contrast to public things because public things are perceivable things and perceivability does not enter into our thought of our own mental phenomena.

This elementary truth about our ability to say what our own beliefs, desires, and so on are is neglected in the philosophy of mind *because* it is conflated with the highly dubious thesis that we have a special introspective access to mental things which, if we did have it, would explain our ability to state our beliefs and other mental states. This explanation has to be carefully distinguished from the fact it tries to explain. The explanation appealing to introspection or some kind of access is a philosopher's thesis. The fact that we can say what we want and what we believe and ordinarily state these matters correctly is a fact, and not a philosophical view at all.

As long as we do not mix up the fact that we can state our own beliefs with popular but insecure philosophical explanations of that fact, we can assure ourselves of the special place of the first-person point of view in the philosophy of mind and in discussion of the concept of belief in particular. The very idea of identity theory is founded on the notion that we know, in the first instance from our own case, that there are such things as beliefs, but we do not yet know what they are. The preliminary familiarity that allegedly generates the demand for an identification is only illustrated by the familiarity a believer has with his own beliefs, the familiarity a perceiver has with his own perceptual experiences, a sufferer's familiarity with his own pains.

The subject matter that needs identifying is essentially the subject matter of first-person reports.

3. Mental phenomena not part of the physical order

The fact that each of us knows about but does not perceive his own mental states and processes is fundamentally connected with the pretheoretical idea that mental things are not constituents of the material order. Descartes called the material order *res extensa*, drawing attention to the fact that it is essentially spatial. Perception is our window on this spatial order. Perceived things are all somewhere in space, and they are spatially locatable with respect to one another. There are many things in the spatial-perceivable realm that are not perceivable, such as atoms and gravitational fields, but, as empiricists have always taught, our knowledge of these things derives from knowledge of things that are accessible to the senses. Similarly, there are nonphysical things which are assigned locations in the spatial-physical order, things like glares, shadows, empty regions, and perhaps surfaces and boundaries. These are allocated to the spatial order because of their connections with physical things which are the primary objects of perception.

In contrast, our thinking about perceptual experiences, beliefs, intentions, desires, and so on, does not include any idea of a spatial location for these things, nor does the knowledge of them that we do have naturally incline us to ascribe any spatial or physical character to these things.

Perhaps because it is one among our mental phenomena and, at the same time, it is anchored in the physical world, perception is an exception to the separateness of the mental and the spatial. No sophisticated scientific or philosophical thought is needed to locate perception in a system of physical conditions and processes. In one mode or another, perception depends upon the availability of light, on having the object of perception in one's mouth, on electrochemical events in nerve tissues, on not being in a vacuum, and on the absence of obstacles (in different senses for the different perceptual modes.) In spite of the dense network of connections between perception and the physical order, perceptual experiences themselves are no more projected into this physical world than are beliefs and intentions. My visual experiences of lemons and tomatoes are not thought of as colored or bulgy things, or as locatable somewhere in the space in which fruits and vegetables are themselves to be found. Our ability to talk about our own perceptual experiences does not include an inclination to assign any physical or sensuous features at all to those experiences. Of course, this is not to deny that perceptual experience inclines us to assign physical and sensuous features, as well as spatial location, to objects perceived.

4. Innerness

Mental things enter into our knowledge and discourse although we do not perceive them, we do not locate them anywhere in space, and we do not assign any sensuous or physical characteristics to them. This is what underlies the intuitive idea that mental things are not part of the material order of things. The philosophical thought that mental things are *inner* is derived from the intuition that mental states and processes are not anywhere out there in the realm of perceived objects, all of which have to be somewhere, and have to be somewhere with respect to one another.

The interior of the human body is *outer* in the sense in which mental things are thought to be inner. Things inside the body have physical and sensuous features, they are perceivable apart from the practical problem of their concealment beneath the opaque surfaces of the body, and they are located in the same space as things outside the body. Therefore, if we adhere to the sense in which mental things are supposed inner in the first place, it is not feasible to construe "inner" as "inside the body."

This modest point is the source of significant confusions. In itself the concept of innerness and the contrast "inner/outer" belong to the vocabulary of spatiality. "Inner" is as spatial as "outer." But as applied to mental things, "inner" is a tricky metaphor. Materialists try to take metaphorical innerness for literal innerness, disregarding the only motives philosophers have ever had for thinking that mental things are inner in the first place. When a philosopher reflects that a perceptual experience is not something that might be on the table or in his shirt pocket, he also thinks that a perceptual experience is not something that could be inside his body: in his nostril, in his stomach, or in his brain. I do not mean this as a refutation of the materialist philosophy of mind. It is, however, a mark of confusion when a materialist, such as Smart, purports to accept the idea that mental things are inner and then goes on to construe that innerness in a spatial sense that allows neural items to count as appropriately inner.

The idea that the mental is not spatial spawns a further confusion in the thinking of Cartesian dualists. Even the dualist innerness that surpasseth all location goes beyond the naive thought that mental things are not part of the material order. Making mental things *inner* assigns them to a hypothetical realm which is built, albeit negatively, on the model of spatial and perceivable things. It is as though, as a first step, philosophers feel secure in the thought that though mental states may not be in the spatial realm of material things, they have to be somewhere!

There is an obvious tension here. The inner becomes a kind of quasi-space *in* which ideas, beliefs, thoughts, and the other elements of mental life can be thought to exist. Thus, materialists who take the metaphor of innerness literally are following the path first prepared by the dualists who also had trouble thinking that mental things are not anywhere at all. For the dualists did think mental things have to be somewhere, namely, *"in* the mind." From this perspective materialists merely assert that the inner quasi-space posited by dualists is not really any different from the space of material things.

The confusions over this point probably come from the prominence of perceptual experiences in the thinking of the dualist philosophers who wanted to segregate the mental and the physical for epistemological and, in the case of Descartes himself, for scientific reasons. This emerges when we remind ourselves of the viewpoint on reality that is supposed to be attained at the high-water mark of Descartes' skepticism. The existence of the "external world" is in doubt, but the indubitable truth of the *cogito* secures the mental life of the thinker as long as he merely contemplates what he finds in consciousness. In Descartes' thinking, this leaves him familiar with a wholly nonspatial reality, since the external that he does not know is precisely the spatial, and, as we have remarked, this spatial world includes the body and all of its contents. From the vantage point of the *cogito* Descartes has to prove the existence of space itself, and not merely of the occupants of space.

This familiar movement of thought is much more complicated in its implications for thinking about spatiality than is generally recognized. Perhaps space is not part of the reality with which we are familiar when we contemplate the contents of the mind, following Descartes' lead. These very mental contents, however, certainly do acquaint us with a realm of application for all kinds of spatial conceptions. The visual experiences we have are only describable in spatial terms. When I contemplate the skeptical proviso "Of course there may be no such thing there outside the mind," I am still left with spatial things *in the mind.* Images of objects which survive doubts about the outer are items filling a system of mutually locatable things. There is a clear sense in which, when Macbeth hallucinates a dagger "handle to my hand," the spatial relations presupposed by this description do obtain in the realm of experience, whether or not there is any dagger, any hand, or even a physical world. This generates the idea of inner space, or private space, and that, in turn, generates the epistemological project that raises questions about the similarities between my private space and the outer space of material things, if any. Perhaps this passage of thought in which private space is "inner" and the space of material objects "outer" illustrates most plainly the strains placed on the concept of the inner in the philosophy of mind. As a consequence of perceptual experiences which are contents of the mind, we are constrained to say that things are located with respect to one another in the inner mental realm as well as in the outer or external world.

This duplication of spatiality in the mind does not really give any footing to the idea that beliefs or desires or perceptual experiences might be located somewhere. The incongruity of the notion that my belief might be under the refrigerator is matched by the equal incongruity of the notion that my belief might be under the image of the refrigerator which I encounter in my visual experience. The intrinsic spatiality of the contents of visual experience does not give footing to the thought that Macbeth's hallucinatory experience of a dagger might lie in some direction from that dagger-image, and might be found at some distance from it, measured, perhaps, in hallucinated dagger-lengths.

The same confusing propensity to duplicate the outer in the mental realm affects our thinking about the sensuous character of things. We suppose in our prephilosophical thinking that mental things like beliefs and desires cannot have sensuous features like color or sound. The inner mental realm becomes one that contrasts with the perceivable realm of things that do have sensuous character. But the skeptical viewpoint so widely adopted since Descartes holds that perceptual experiences are not threatened by the nonexistence of the outer world. The sensuous features of perceived objects then reappear as features of experiences themselves. The redness of the hallucinated apple is not repudiated along with the existence of the external object. The mental realm comes to contain a duplicate or parallel sensuous reality as well as a duplicate spatial order. Following a pattern of ironic reversals, versions of the traditional theory of secondary qualities go on to make the mind the *only* home of sensuous qualities, while the true nature of the outer is captured in nonsensuous mathematical representations.

But once again the understanding of perception which brings sensuous features into the realm of the mental does nothing whatever to make it plausible that beliefs and desires might have sensuous character. Just as plainly, though perceptual experiences are *of sensuously described things*, the sensuous finds no field of application to perceptual experiences.

Finally, the thought of innerness is a device by which concepts of mental items such as beliefs and desires retain their status as realities to which reference can be made. In contemporary discussions the concept of a sake, as in, for example, "For my friend's sake, I hope that . . . ," has become a standard illustration for nonreferential status. My friend's sake is not locatable anywhere and has no physical or sensuous character. But we have no inclination to add sakes to the roster of inner realities. This is because we do not think of sakes as having any existence at all. Things that exist can be referred to. Beliefs and desires fall into this category, while sakes do not. So we think that a metaphysical home must be found for mental states and processes because we think of them as suitable objects for reference. Neither my friend's sake nor his belief that interest rates will fall are located at any distance at all from the Federal Reserve Bank, but his belief is a reality of some kind, while his sake is not. Thus we arrive at the idea that his belief must be an inner reality.

From this point of view there is no further step needed to reach the conviction that this reality — my friend's belief that interest rates will fall — must have some constitution or other. We must be entitled to an answer to the question

> What are these strange mental things that we can refer to and know about and, yet, that seem not to belong to the physical order of things?

A philosophical view that answers this question will be a philosophy of mind in the form of an identity theory. Such a theory will say that this belief and all other beliefs and desires together with all other mental states and processes of all creatures with mental lives are actually (a) modifications of a nonmaterial mind-stuff of which such creatures are in part composed, or (b) neural states or processes in the nervous systems of such creatures, or (c) functional states of such creatures (or machines) defined in terms of their functional rôles, which are defined, in turn, in terms of causes and effects, or (d) . . . . The blank theory (d) leaves room for a further, as yet unenvisioned, philosophical identity theory.

I am quite convinced that the move from the naive exclusion of mental things from the realm of the spatial, the material, and the perceivable to the philosophical idea of an inner range of realities in need of a metaphysical identification is a mistake. People know about their own beliefs and the rest of their mental states in the sense that they can assert with confidence and with a generally conceded authority things such as "I believe that interest rates are going to fall" and "I want a raise in pay." If I have this belief and this desire, then, of course, my belief and my desire are realities as long as that just means that I *do* believe that interest rates are going to fall and I *do* desire a raise in pay. In this sense everyone knows that mental things are real. But no one but a philosopher takes this much as a foundation for a demand for the constitution of this belief and this desire.

Is my belief itself a physical state or process, contrary to naive convictions? Or, failing that, is my belief something nonphysical, perhaps a spiritual state or shadowy process that occurs *in* some mysterious nonmaterial part of my constitution? Confidence that I really do believe that interest rates are going to fall is not confidence that these philosophical questions must be addressed. The idea that we should ask for an identification of belief, that is, ask what it is, what constitutes it, and to what metaphysical status we should allocate it, is an idea that belongs only to philosophical thought. No such idea is part of the truism that people do have beliefs. Maybe philosophers are right, and these things are inner phenomena that require to be identified by philosophers of mind. We cannot reject identity theory by merely noting the limits of our ordinary thinking in the absence of such theory. Neither can we suppose that the philosophical identification project is already set in motion by the mere appreciation that we do have beliefs, desires, and experience.

5. The contrast: pretheoretical notions and philosophical ideas

I have been making appeal to naive intuition in the honorific spirit which eighteenth-century romantics reserved for noble savages. This appeal will understandably arouse skepticism. Who is to say what our pretheoretical views about the mental are? Is everyone supposed to recognize the same division between the straight thinking of plain men and opinions contaminated by philosophical reflection? Why not suppose that intelligent reflection might improve our naive thoughts instead of assuming that it will inevitably make them worse? How could a dispute about whether a particular view belongs to the roster of prephilosophical thought be resolved? In particular, I have said that a shared intuitive standpoint finds that mental things are not part of the physical world, but that the same naïveté does not assign mental things to a nonphysical status. Is not this rather too delicate an opinion to discern in prephilosophical thinking?

I will certainly not propose a theory for the identification of the nontheoretical. A general methodology is not required here. I have no plans to use these intuitive thoughts as premises. I accept the supposition that any naive opinion can be quite false and can be improved on or rejected when tested by reflection at a sophisticated and theoretical level. We are interested in only a few nontheoretical ideas here. I am not promoting common sense as a warehouse of metaphysical truths, and I am not espousing a democratic philosophy that would try to "think with the vulgar." The strategy of argument that I do propose is as follows: Philosophers thinking about mental concepts take the starting point of their investigations to be somewhat beyond anything definitely suggested by prephilosophical thoughts about mental things. I say that this advance beyond naive thinking consists in the assumption that mental phenomena are inner realities of some kind or other. I want to secure agreement that this is a little step beyond natural intuitions, because that will motivate questioning the reasonableness of the little step. In trying to answer that question, once it is motivated, I aim to show that theories construing mental phenomena as inner realities cannot possibly do the job that is envisioned for them. This is the *argument* against the inner-state interpretation of mental phenomena. The ultimate rejection of inner-state theories about particular mental phenomena is founded on incoherences they are shown to contain and not on the fact that we have no commitment to inner states among our pretheoretical conceptions of mentality.

The first stage-setting considerations are worth our trouble precisely because the view that mental phenomena *must be* inner realities of some kind is so very widely and confidently held among philosophers. Now that behaviorism is no longer endorsed by many philosophers of mind, a conviction that either some version of materialist identity theory (including functionalism as one version)[3] or some form of the unattractive Cartesian dualism must be correct is almost universal among philosophers. Of course, this would be true if mental phenomena were inner realities of some kind. Logic alone moves us from that proposition to the conclusion that they must be either inner physical realities or inner nonphysical realities, since physical and nonphysical exhaustively partition the domain of inner realities on any theory.

In the atmosphere of philosophical thought that starts from a confident acceptance of inner states and processes, ineliminable mysteries in the resulting identity theories are perceived as "problems" that must be solvable somehow. The evaluation of the overall explanatory potential of any such theory is replaced by a technical development addressed to points of detail which lead away from the broad issues that arise as soon as the feasibility of *any* inner-reality theory is investigated. Therefore, if it is possible to show that the inner reality of mental phenomena is not a commitment of prephilosophical thinking, or even if it is possible to show that this may be so, it is very much worth our while to try to do it.

At the present time the gradual spread of appreciation of the difficulties facing materialism, such as the problem of accounting for *qualia* and the issues surrounding the necessity of true identity statements raised by Saul Kripke,* is fostering the beginnings of a revival

---

*Kripke himself appears to think of these problems as an indication of the superiority of a Cartesian philosophy of mind. See *Naming and Necessity*, Cambridge, Massachusetts, 1980, Third Lecture. Chapter 5, below, contains an examination of Kripke's views insofar as they impinge on the philosophy of mind and on identity theory in particular. The discovery of these problems that stand in the way of a materialist identity theory is, at least in part, the rediscovery of the reasons for which dualists did not think it possible that mental things could be material in the first place. That these old reasons need to be rediscovered is mostly a consequence of the fact that materialism is always supported mainly by the global conviction that dualism *has to be* wrong. This conviction engenders an optimistic materialist program in the name of science. But it offers no guidance at all when the old reasons for rejecting materialism are rearticulated. Far more important, in my opinion, is the thought that

of dualism. This is the consequence of the idea that philosophers are forced to choose between materialism and dualism. The inner-reality interpretation of mental phenomena creates the necessity of this choice. The viability of that interpretation is the crucial issue throughout this investigation.

In the absence of any guidelines as to what is and what is not naive thought about the mental we have to think naively about each particular view. The broad legitimacy of the contrast between the intuitive and the theoretical is not really open to dispute. Concerning belief, for example, there is a conspicuous difference between the idea that I do have beliefs, that others are also believers, and that some beliefs are true and some are false, on the one hand, and the contention that beliefs are neural states of believers, or functional states, or states of the immortal souls of believers, on the other. It is entirely understandable that philosophers should think that opinions of the latter sort may turn out to be correct. These opinions do, however, have their theoretical status on the surface. It takes a theorist of some kind, philosophical or scientific, to think that our beliefs are neural states. The mere idea that we have beliefs, that we talk about them, and that they can be true or false is not part of any theory.

I am interested in the intermediate view that goes beyond the patently naive appreciation that we do have beliefs and falls short of the identification of beliefs with some specific inner reality of a particular metaphysical category. The intermediate view is the thought that beliefs are inner things of *some kind*. Here we should not simply try to test the feel of this proposition, each of us using his own measure for degree of naïveté. Rather we have to consider precisely what the knowledge that we do have beliefs comes to. In this connection we have pointed out that beliefs are not objects of perception, and this is an important part of our willingness to think of them as not part of the order of physical things. Again I have said that we do not have any naive convictions about how it is that we know about our own

---

the dualist hypothesis that mental phenomena might be identifiable with realities in a certain substance (nonmaterial substance) is retained by the materialists who merely substitute material substance while adhering to the format of identification. Since the dualist's exotic identification was initially motivated by an appreciation of the impossibility of a materialist identification, the indicated correction of dualism is the repudiation of identity theory as the form for philosophy of mind.

beliefs and are able to state them upon demand. But *we do know about them and we can state them*. We have no conviction that we ought to describe this ability in terms of an inner thing which we consult and report on. I stress that we are not secure about what to say. We do not intuitively reject out of hand the suggestion that in knowing our belief we apprehend an inner item. Nor do we intuitively insist on this conception. This indefiniteness is the phenomenological situation. I am asked, "What do you think about interest rates? How will they move?" I reply, "I believe rates are going to come down." How did I proceed here? No intuitively compelling answer to this inquiry comes to mind.

The idea that our beliefs are inner realities seems to me to be incontestably of a different order from the idea that we do have beliefs and that some are true and others false. If I am right about this, we should be much more cautious than philosophers commonly are in adopting the inner-reality interpretation of mental phenomena.

6. Behaviorism

The claim that mental life is not constituted of a range of inner realities is already familiar in behaviorist thinking. It is customary to distinguish between methodological behaviorism and philosophical or analytical behaviorism. Methodological behaviorism takes no stand on inner mental realities. It merely emphasizes the principle that scientific understanding has to rest entirely on appeal to matters that are publicly observable. Thus, mental phenomena which are intuitively thought of as private ought to be excluded from the evidential basis of psychology. For the moment we are concerned only with the latter behaviorism, that is, with analytical behaviorism, which rejects inner mental states and processes, not because they are not accessible for public scrutiny, but because there are no such things to be scrutinized.

Philosophical behaviorists attempt an analytical reduction of mental concepts to concepts of dispositions, all of the manifestations of which are publicly observable behavior. This radical project has not got many adherents left, and I do not think it gets very much right in its treatment of mental phenomena. At one time it was accepted by some leading thinkers and taken very seriously by many more. This fact alone makes behaviorism interesting and pertinent to our preliminary consideration of mental concepts. The very fact of the existence of behaviorism as a philosophy of mind and its possession of a real following at one time shows us something important about our concepts of mental phenomena.

I should say that our knowledge of our beliefs, sensations, perceptual experiences, and desires is at least as prominent in our ordinary lives as is our knowledge of our physical constitution described in nontheoretical terms. A philosopher proposing that our ordinary convictions about our inner physical constitution are systematically erroneous—for example, our conviction that there are teeth in our jaws and that there is blood in our veins—could not be taken seriously or attract a following. Any effort to "analyze the concepts of teeth and blood" in a way that denies that there are any such things could not be the import of a theory that leading thinkers might espouse and debate. But the claim that equally familiar beliefs, desires, sensations, and perceptual experiences, are not inner realities at all can be intelligibly espoused and has in fact been subjected to serious consideration and debate by sober thinkers. It would be silly to argue that this *de facto* tolerance of the very idea of behaviorism shows that behaviorism is right and that mental things are not inner realities. Serious debate of behaviorist hypotheses does show that our thinking is insecure about mental phenomena in a sense in which thinking about teeth and blood is not insecure. The behaviorist hypothesis is something that manages to coexist with our ordinary knowledge of mental things because that ordinary knowledge consists in knowing that John loves Mary, that Sally intends to quit her job, that George has a headache, and that I believe that interest rates are going to fall. Where inner states come into this ordinary knowledge, or if inner states come into it at all, is not something that is also clear to ordinary people who know about these matters.

Of course, there is such a thing as consciousness and self-consciousness. Ideas about self-consciousness are part of naive thinking about the mental. But, in the absence of theories the concepts of consciousness that we have do not necessarily require us to speak of inner things or goings-on. "I am conscious of my dislike of Edgar" may just mean that I know I dislike Edgar without giving the question any special thought or analysis. Maybe consciousness means much more than this.

Maybe, in my mental life, I do introspect, that is, I look into something, as it were, and find things like my beliefs and perceptual experiences, on which I am then able to report. It is not obvious that this is so, as it is obvious that I do have teeth in my jaws. There is something unsettled about our conception of mental things. We are not merely insecure as to whether inner realities we do know about are physical or nonphysical realities. In one sense everything is easy. But that is only the sense in which I know that John loves Mary and that I believe that interest rates will fall. This sense does not give me a conviction that mental things are inner phenomena of some kind or other.

That is why behaviorists are not hooted down. They can be taken seriously because we appreciate that we have no very solid idea about what mental states are, or even whether that is a question we should be asking about them. If mental things were the familiar things of inner reality that identity theorists take for granted that they are, then we would all know that, as we all know that teeth are objects in our mouths. If mental things had a status like that, we could not take a behaviorist seriously. His would be a lunatic philosophy of mind, not a debatable theory. He would be like a man telling us that there are no pots and pans in the kitchen when we know perfectly well that there are. To be sure, behaviorism is a radical view, and it does seem to offend intuitive thoughts about the mental. But the offense is much less egregious than it would be if mental states and processes were inner realities with which we are all familiar in the ordinary course of things. We simply have no intuitive conviction that mental things are things that are present in or go on in us at all.

7. Eliminative materialism

The version of materialist philosophy of mind known as "eliminative materialism" also rejects the idea that beliefs and desires are inner realities needing to be identified. According to this philosophy of mind the concepts of mental phenomena can be brought together under the rather pejorative title "folk psychology." These concepts belong to a prescientific understanding of things, and they need not generate an identity theory because, from a viewpoint sufficiently enlightened by science, there are no such things to be identified. This doctrine comes close to the offense to everyday intuition which I have said behaviorism avoids. For this contention amounts to the idea that mental concepts like belief and desire figure only in unsuccessful explanatory hypotheses.

Expositions of this point of view commonly assimilate the concepts of folk psychology to concepts of demons and witches that belong to superstitious or fictional explanatory projects. Terms that purport to refer to demons and witches never succeed in referring to such things, since there are none of them, so we no longer use these concepts in the context of explanation. If there were demons, demons would have to have some nature, however supernatural. An identity theory would explicate the nature of demons and assign them to their proper metaphysical status as physical or nonphysical entities. From a scientific point of view an identity theory for beliefs and desires is no more to be expected than an identity theory for demons. This eliminativist thesis violates common sense in that it discredits all explanations that invoke beliefs and desires. It entails that "Sally wants a raise in pay" and "I believe that interest rates will fall" are false together with all other assertions about the mental states that are *eliminated*.

This looms as a lunatic philosophy of mind, as behaviorism does not, because it does not merely attack the thought that beliefs and desires are inner realities (which is an insecure thought and not an intuitive conviction), but it also attacks the idea that people have beliefs and desires, which seems to be an ineliminable truth and a truth which is not attacked by analytical behaviorism. The only excuse for this outrageous thesis is that it stems from a recognition that mental phenomena are not going to be identified successfully by *any* theory. Having accepted the mistaken preliminary notion that beliefs and the like would have to be inner realities of some kind, the eliminative materialist heroically, if ill-advisedly, concludes that there are no beliefs at all, that no one actually believes anything. The defect of the theory lies in the assumption that beliefs have to be inner things calling for an identity. The eliminative theory resulting from this mistake is a perverse philosophy of mind, although it is understandable that it is an opinion espoused at a university and not merely at an asylum.

8. Philosophical resistance to the idea of inner mental things

Many philosophers and psychologists have developed critical views about the inner-reality interpretation of mental phenomena. My own understandings in the philosophy of mind are heavily indebted to those thinkers. I say this not only in acknowledgment of their inspiration and influence but also to moderate an appearance of excessive originality in the views presented here. Originality in philosophy shades insensibly into crankiness. The views I will defend here go against ideas that are widely taken for granted. But I do not think that there is any crankiness in the claims I will make.

By far the most important precedent for rejection of the inner-state or inner-process interpretation of mental concepts and the largest influence on my thinking is that of Wittgenstein. At *Philosophical Investigations* #305 Wittgenstein is dealing with questions that arise out of his celebrated remarks about pain, reports of pain, and pain behavior.* He faces the thought that his understanding seems to deny that something inner takes place. He introduces the concept of remembering as a partially parallel topic. Is not remembering an inner process on which we report? And is not an understanding like the one he has been promoting in the context of pain equivalent to the denial that there is any inner process of remembering? At this point Wittgenstein says,

> The impression that we wanted to deny something arises from our setting our faces against the picture of an "inner process."

And taking up the same theme at #306:

> Why should I deny that there is a mental process? But "There has just taken place in me the mental process of remembering . . . ," means nothing more than "I have just remembered. . . ." To deny the mental process would mean to deny the remembering, to deny that anyone ever remembers anything.

The last sentence of this citation is the view actually reached by eliminative materialists.

Finally, at #308 we find the culmination of this theme in what is an unusually explicit statement by Wittgenstein.

> How does the philosophical problem about mental processes and states and behaviorism arise? — The first step is the one that altogether escapes

---

*I do not mean that I endorse or even understand Wittgenstein's statement about pains. As a matter of fact, I think that pains are inner realities located in the bodies but not in the brains (at least not ordinarily) of sufferers.

notice. We talk of processes and states and leave their nature undecided. Sometime perhaps we shall know more about them—we think. But this is just what commits us to a particular way of looking at the matter. For we have a definite concept of what it means to know a process better. The decisive movement in the conjuring trick has been made, and it was the very one that we thought quite innocent.

Wittgenstein is making explicit our philosophical habits of thought when he says, "But 'There has just occurred in me the mental process of remembering. . . ,' means nothing more than 'I have just remembered.' " The longer and more awkward formulation seems to be only a restatement. On the strength of the restatement, however, we "talk of processes and leave their nature undecided." Their nature would be decided by an identity theory concerning memory. If I did remember that p, then *remembering that p* did take place. *I* did the remembering, so it did not take place in someone else or anywhere outside of me. It took place *in* me, in some sense. This seems somewhat artificial, and at the same time, since the formulation in terms of a process of remembering seems to be mere restatement, the inner-reality interpretation appears to be inevitable and undiscussable.

The longer and somewhat artificial "There has just occurred in me the mental process of remembering . . ." has a theoretical cast that the idiomatic "I just remembered . . ." does not have at all. We do not seem to have changed the content in the restatement, and yet, as restated, we are entitled to wonder about the character of the inner process of remembering and its metaphysical standing. Is it not the case that the transition to the "restatement" has introduced an inner item that is not in any obvious way a commitment of "I just remembered"? We have to bring into the open the transition from the naive to the theoretical that goes by so smoothly here.

The conjurer of Wittgenstein's #308 is not Descartes or the materialist philosophers of mind who set themselves the job of identifying inner realities and allocating them to their appropriate metaphysical categories. These philosophers are, rather, among the victims of the illusion that gets us to accept without reflection the idea that memory, belief, desire, and perceptual experience must be states and processes of some kind—if not outer, then inner—if not physical, then nonphysical.

NOTES

1. For this favorable judgment by a contemporary consider, for example, Jerry Fodor's conception of the "representational theory of mind," which he endorses and in which he recognizes affinity with the classical philosophy of mind that is essentially that devised by Descartes and adopted by the classical tradition of British empiricism. The idea of the privacy of the mental reappears in Fodor's thinking in his conception of "methodological solipsism." See chapter 9, "Methodological Solipsism Considered as a Research Strategy in Cognitive Psychology," in Fodor, *Representations*, Cambridge, Massachusetts, 1981. Fodor's acceptance of the Cartesian perspective is exceptional only in its explicitness. Part of the value of Fodor's work on this point is to bring into open discussion a traditional conception which operates without express acknowledgment in the thinking of a great many contemporary philosophers of mind.

2. J. J. C. Smart, "Materialism," *J. Phil.*, LX, 1963; as reprinted in C. V. Borst, *The Mind-Brain Identity Theory*, London, 1972, p. 162.

3. Some functionalists have proposed that their view is compatible with dualism in that a nonmaterial state might, in principle, satisfy the causal definition of a functional state. See, for example, H. Putnam, "Philosophy and Our Mental Life," in *Philosophical Papers*, Cambridge, 1975, vol. II, pp. 291-303. Nonetheless functionalism is generally taken to be a version of materialist philosophy of mind. The idea that functional states might not be physical would have the obvious disadvantage of reintroducing into metaphysics all of the intractable mysteries of mind-body interaction.

II

Belief Statements and Belief States

1. Ascriptions and expressions of belief

It is harder than it looks to say just what is conveyed by statements like "Joe believes that the cat is on the mat" and "I believe that the cat is on the mat." The possibility of difficulty here is well known to philosophers under the heading of the opacity of belief contexts, and in discussions of *de re* versus *de dicto* belief. But I have in mind more elementary considerations.

Let us call third-person statements like "Joe believes that the cat is on the mat" *ascriptions* of belief, and first-person statements like "I believe that the cat is on the mat" *expressions* of belief. It is clear enough that ascriptions of belief that p are not assertions of p, whatever it is that they do assert. The speaker who says, "Joe believes that the cat is on the mat," takes no stand on the location of the cat in ascribing this belief to Joe. He himself may know where the cat is, or he may have a good idea, or none at all. He need not address the question of the cat's whereabouts in order to pronounce on what is plainly a wholly different matter, namely, Joe's belief that the cat is on the mat.

Although this much is transparently clear, it is worthwhile to note that the same independence of an ascription of belief and the belief ascribed is visible at once in the pattern of truth values that the ascription and the belief itself may take. Thus, "The cat is on the mat" is true, if, and only if, the cat *is* on the mat, but "Joe believes the cat is on the mat" may be true even if the cat is not on the mat. And with equal obviousness, "Joe believes that the cat is on the mat" may be false, in case Joe has no such belief, even though "The cat is on the mat" is true. If we were minded to make a principle out of what is obvious here, we could state it thus:

> The Assertion Principle: If a statement q is an assertion of
> p, then q is true, if, and only if, p is true.

An ascription of belief that p is not an assertion of p. This conforms
with the platitudinous Assertion Principle. Our motives for this concern with the obvious emerge gradually when we consider expressions
of belief.

It seems natural to suppose that when Joe says, "I believe that
p," he is saying of himself just what another says of him in saying,
"Joe believes that p." Just as the ascriber does not assert p in his ascription but rather makes a statement about Joe which is true or false
whether or not p, so too Joe appears to make a statement about himself,
and when he says, "I believe that p," he does not assert p but makes
a statement which has truth conditions quite other than those of p.
Certainly, "I believe that p" is not accounted false on the ground that
p is false, and is not true because p is true. The Assertion Principle
assures us that expressions of belief that p do not assert that p any
more than ascriptions do.

This much is impressed upon us by very simple considerations,
so simple that I have had to apologize for putting into words what
is so evident to everyone. Yet what appears to be evident is, in fact,
mistaken. We can encourage a sense that something is wrong here by
reflecting on the scope of the disclaimer: In an expression of belief
that p, a speaker is not asserting p. We saw that an ascriber takes no
stand on the truth or falsehood of the belief itself but merely says
something about the believer. That the cat is on the mat is something
which the ascriber may also be willing to assert or deny, or he may
not be willing to take any stand on this further topic. Can this really
be the outlook for Joe himself when he tells us that he believes that p?
If so, Joe could say,

> I take no stand on p itself. That is another question. The
> whereabouts of the cat is something about which I remain
> neutral and uncommitted. I say only that I believe that the
> cat is on the mat.

When we ask Joe where he thinks the cat is, we cannot suppose that
he answers appropriately if he does not address the whereabouts of
the cat in his answer. He cannot set that issue aside as something else
about which he might or might not also make an assertion. We might

ask about his belief in the question, "Do you think that the statement 'The cat is on the mat' is true or false?" Surely he cannot answer *this* question while remaining uncommitted on the whereabouts of the cat and while taking no stand on the truth of "The cat is on the mat" itself.

If Joe says, "I believe that the cat is on the mat," we cannot ask him, "What about the cat's location, would you say anything on that subject too?" He cannot go on at this point, to assert that the cat is actually on the mat, any more than he can go on to assert that the cat is not on the mat.* We said above that the ascriber and Joe make the same statement in the third and first person, respectively. But the ascriber can go on to say, on p itself, that the cat is on the mat, or that it is not on the mat. Joe cannot do this because his "I believe that the cat is on the mat" expresses his stand on "The cat is on the mat." His expression of belief is a way of saying that "The cat is on the mat" is true. Then it is a way of saying that the cat is on the mat. It asserts the belief it expresses. But that cannot be right for it violates the Assertion Principle.

First we thought that, like an ascription, an expression of belief does not assert the belief. Then, mindful of the fact that "I believe that p" indicates the speaker's stand on p itself, we thought that expressions do assert the belief. But we must have moved improperly to this conclusion since it is flatly excluded by the Assertion Principle.

Can we explain the character of Joe's discourse without supposing that his "I believe that p" asserts p? As everyone knows, those who believe that p will generally assert that p when the question of the

---

*The discussion at this point is certain to bring to mind Moore's so called "paradox," namely, the conjunction "I believe that p, and it is not the case that p." Moore said that this conjunction is "absurd" though not contradictory. It is not contradictory, he thought, in that each of the conjuncts may be true, though their joint assertion is absurd. Moore's brief discussions of this issue do not contain any philosophical account of the alleged paradox and do not go into the question of the assertive force of expressions of belief. Since, as I will argue, "I belief that p" is an assertion of p, the conjunction is actually a curiously stated contradiction, and there is nothing paradoxical in the fact that it cannot be properly asserted. For Moore's statements on the topic see "Russell's Theory of Descriptions," in P. Schillp, *The Philosophy of Bertrand Russell*, Evanston, Illinois, 1944, p. 203; and G. E. Moore, *Philosophical Papers*, London, 1959, pp. 173-74. See also M. Black, "Saying and Disbelieving," *Analysis*, V, 13, 1952; and J. Hintikka, *Knowledge and Belief*, Ithaca, New York, 1962, pp. 9, 64ff, and 95-102.

truth or falsehood of p arises. Believing that p is the best of reasons
for asserting that p. When Joe has told us that he believes that p, we
will not ask him what he says about p itself because we know that those
who believe that p will assert that p. We can ask the ascriber what
he thinks about p itself because he has not been identified as one who
believes that p. "I believe that p" says something about the believer
and does not assert p, but it implies that the speaker will also assert
that p and take the stand "It is true" on p itself. That is why we cannot, without deviance of some kind, ask, "What about the location
of the cat?" when Joe has just asserted, "I believe that the cat is on
the mat." In asserting, "I believe that p," Joe does not say what stand
he takes on p itself, although he does indicate what he would say about
that.

But this explanation cannot be right. Having asserted, "Joe believes that the cat is on the mat," the ascriber can be asked, "And
where is the cat? Would you say anything on that issue?" But we cannot suppose that the ascriber could be asked, "And what stand does
Joe take on the whereabouts of the cat? Or does he take any stand
on that?" The ascription of belief says what *Joe's* stand is on p itself.
It does not tell us the speaker's stand on p, but this is because the
speaker is not the believer. In an expression of belief *the speaker is
the believer.* Joe cannot say of himself what an ascriber of belief says
of him without thereby committing himself on p itself. For what the
ascriber says of Joe is that he is committed to the truth of p. We need
not look far for explanation of the fact that we cannot ask a speaker
for his stand on p itself when he has expressed belief that p. The
minimal explanation here is the correct one: the speaker has just told
us what his stand on p itself is. Therefore, in accepting Joe's "I believe that p," we do not have a foundation for the expectation that
Joe will also say that p is itself true. His "I believe that p" *asserts* this
stand on p itself, just as the ascription asserts of Joe that this is his
stand on p.

Does this mean that an expression of belief is merely an assertion of the belief expressed after all? That is excluded by the Assertion Principle. The pattern of truth values for "I believe that p" and
p are different. It looks now as though we need a very subtle distinction between asserting p, on the one hand, and indicating how one
answers the question "Is p true or false?" or "Are you committed to
the truth of p?" on the other. Telling others how I am committed,

or how I answer certain questions, or what stand I take on something, still carries the flavor of communication about the speaker. Therefore, any of these statements seems to contain information about the speaker that is not contained in the unadorned assertion "The cat is on the mat." And there can be no doubt that the cat's being on the mat *is one thing* and my believing it *is another*. There ought to be a form of words in which I can give expression to the latter and not just the former matter of fact.

Upon reflection, the expectation that I should be able to state the fact that I believe that p somehow, without asserting that p, turns out to be empty. It is merely a resurgence of the idea that we have just examined. For if we do provide Joe with a means of expressing the fact that he holds the belief that p without saying anything on p itself, then another will be right to say of Joe just what he says of himself. That other would not say what determination Joe makes about p itself, since that is not what Joe says. But this is nonsense. An ascriber of belief that p to Joe has to say what Joe's determination on p itself is. That is the whole point of an ascription of belief. No other information about Joe will do.

What about the indisputable fact that my believing that p is one thing and p being the case is something else again? Since they are plainly different, why can I not state merely the first? Perhaps this is less paradoxical than it seems. Obviously I can address the question "Is it the case that p?" and do my best to resolve that question definitively. Having finished my work on that matter of fact, finding that it is the case that p, or, perhaps, that it is not, I can hardly move on to the question "Do I believe that p?" From another's point of view these two questions can be separately investigated, but not from mine. So when we insist that there is a difference between S's believing that p and it being that case that p, it is no wonder that we have not called attention to matters that S could investigate separately. If he finds that p is true, he has to say, "I believe that p." Of course, he may be wrong, and then p will be false even though he investigates, takes p to be true, and expresses the appropriate belief. Someone else may be right or wrong about two different questions: Is it the case that p? and Does S believe that p? The fact that S may be right or wrong in his finding on the first question does not indicate that there are two separate questions for S here. Surely there are not.

Furthermore, this consideration makes it appear that an expression of belief is not a report in which the speaker tells others about himself. It seems that the speaker does not speak of a state that is present in himself even though what he says bears restatement in the third person as a statement about him. When S investigates the question "Is it the case that p?" and resolves that issue about the world affirmatively, he need not carry out any further investigation of himself or note anything present in or going on in him at all in order to be fully justified in telling others, "I believe that p." Finding that p is the case, there is simply no rôle at all for information that the speaker may have or lack concerning his own states in determining what he should say in answer to the enquiry "Do you believe that p?" It is hard to fit an inner subject matter into our picture of expressions of belief at all.

This is confirmed by the fact that the most common and natural vehicle for the expression of belief that p *is* the simple assertion of p and is not a formulation with the prefacing words "I believe that." These words imply insecurity or reservation on the part of the speaker relative to the mere assertion of p. The preface is selected to express this insecurity on p and not to mark the speaker's utterance as an expression of belief. If assertion of p did not express belief that p, it would be feasible, when someone has just asserted, "The cat is on the mat," to ask, "And what about your belief on that point, do you also believe that the cat is on the mat?" Of course we challenge speakers with "Do you believe that?" when they have asserted p. But this challenge relies on the fact that assertion does express belief, since the hostile question is based on taking the speaker's assertion of p to be an expression of belief that p and, furthermore, an ill-advised expression of that belief.

"I believe that p" expresses insecurity relative to the bare assertion of p. Even exceptions illustrate the validity of this rule. At dinner a woman might say "I believe that my husband is alive" if her husband disappeared years earlier. If her husband is among the diners, she cannot make this statement unless it is meant as a rather mean joke. As a joke it only succeeds by implying that her husband's being alive is something about which she might reasonably be uncertain. There is a polite as well as a mean usage in which we can say, exceptionally, "I believe" of things of which we are certain. If I remark, "As Pythagoras said, 'Man is the measure of all things,' " you may offer the polite correction, "I believe that was Protagoras." Courtesy is achieved here by falsely implying that the speaker is uncertain so that another's error should not seem exceptional. Although the speaker does know whereof he speaks, his use of "I believe" ceremonially implies that he does not know.

Now we have to face the Assertion Principle head on. The principle sounds like a truism, but it is not even a truth. It is indisputable that "I believe that p" is not false on the ground that p is false, or true in case p is true. Nonetheless, we have said that "I believe that p" is an assertion of p which differs from p, not in asserted content, but only in the element of insecurity expressed by the prefacing "I believe that." In order to reject the Assertion Principle we have to show there can be a statement q which asserts p, although q is true when p is false. We have to show that expressions of belief such as "I believe that p" are illustrations of such statements.

2. Some help from Austin

There is a further desideratum for the understanding of "I believe that p" that contains a hint for the refutation of the Assertion Principle. We need an understanding of belief which construes expressions of belief as assertions of the belief and construes ascriptions of belief as statements about the believer which do not assert p. This has to be accomplished without introducing two senses for "belief that p": one for ascriptions and another for expressions of belief. We need a single concept that shifts naturally from a statement about the believer to an assertion of p, in the shift from the third to the first person. Only such a concept will make intelligible the logical relations into which ascriptions and expressions of belief enter. The quantified assertion "Someone believes that p" follows equally from "Joe believes that p" and from "I believe that p." The generalization "Everyone who was an eyewitness believes that p" follows from the premises "Joe and I were the only eyewitnesses. Joe believes that p, and I believe that p." These and myriad other logical and conceptual relations militate against any but a univocal understanding of first- and third-person belief statements.

The speech acts that Austin called "performatives" suggest the direction in which we might find what we need by way of a concept of belief.[1] Performatives exhibit the relationships between the first and third person that we are looking for. "Joe promises to pay you tomorrow" asserts something true or false about Joe and does not do any promising. But in saying, "I promise to pay you tomorrow," Joe promises and does not say anything about himself. Joe's speech act creates an obligation, while the ascriber's speech act is merely informative about Joe. But the univocal character of the concept reappears as soon as we reflect that the third person statement says of Joe that he places himself under the very obligation that he does place himself under in the performative speech act. If Joe did say something about himself, if he described himself or reported something he knew to be present in himself, he would not be promising, however correct his information about himself might be. So only in the performative speech act is Joe doing the thing that another person says Joe does with the words "Joe promises."

There are performative speech acts such as "I assert that p" and "I say that p," which are expressions of belief that p. Furthermore these are counterinstances to the Assertion Principle. Saying the words "I assert that p" is asserting that p. Yet, "I assert that p" is not false when p turns out to be false. It is not false because if I assert it, I assert p, and that is what it says I do. But no one could claim to have got things right because of this consideration when p turns out to be false. When he finds that p is false, Joe's "I said 'I assert that p' " will be a concession of error and not a reassertion of something Joe asserted before, and something he was right about. However, although the performative "I assert that p" is suggestive, it is of no use in the analysis of belief. One can say these words, although one does not believe that p. One can believe that p and say nothing.

Austin tried to stretch the idea of performative speech acts to reach "I know." His idea is that I pledge myself and vouch for my doing what I promise to do in saying "I promise," and, in much the same way, I back the truth of p with my credit and I vouch for its truth when I say "I know that p." This is quite unsuccessful and only brings "I know" part way under the rubric of performatives. For a true performative the action is done by saying the words. So saying "I promise to pay tomorrow" is promising to pay tomorrow. Saying "I know that the cat is on the mat" is *not* knowing that the cat is on the mat. It is in significant part because of cases like this that Austin abandoned the concept of performatives in favor of the much more general and flexible idea of illocutionary force. But we need pursue these difficulties facing quasi-performatives no further.

"I believe that p" does make an assertion. It does not require Austin's insights to understand that making assertions is one of the things that we *do* when we speak. I am arguing that the inner-state interpretation misidentifies the assertion that expressions of belief make. Austin is relevant, not because he thought that "I know" can be given a quasi-performative analysis which we might hope to extend to "I believe," but only for his handling of the relationship of first- and third-person discourse. Austin offers paradigms of first-person speech acts, such as Joe's "I promise to pay," which are confusingly like assertions *about the speaker*, Joe, but are actually not assertions at all. I point to Austin's thinking to help overcome the impression that "I believe that p" is an assertion about the speaker without denying that, as a speech act, it is an assertion. It is an assertion of p.

We cannot simply say, as Austin said of "I know," that "I believe" is like a performative in that the speaker uttering these words vouches for the truth of what he asserts. For this is not so. We drew attention to the insecurity that actually motivates the use of the phrase "I believe that." Can a believer not assert that p while acknowledging the possibility of error? Is not that, in fact, just what we do when we express belief that p using the formula "I believe that p?" When we express belief that p without this mark of insecurity, that is, when we say simply that p, it is still the case that we may be mistaken. But "I believe that p" alludes explicitly to the possibility of being wrong in asserting p.

This brings us to the threshold of the solution of both problems we set ourselves: the refutation of the Assertion Principle and the explication of a univocal concept of belief that appears so different in force in its first- and third-person usage. There is a somewhat rhetorical but familiar enough form of words that clearly expresses belief that p, and, like "I believe that p," this form of words directly alludes to the possibility of being mistaken. I refer to

p, or I am much mistaken.

It is clear that the assertive content here is really only p, since the truth value of p is what determines the truth or falsehood of both of the elements disjoined in this assertion. The first disjunct is p, and it has, in consequence, the truth value of p. The second disjunct is intended as the claim that as one who takes the stand that p is true, I will be mistaken if p is false. Of course, if I assert just p, without this curious appendage, I am mistaken if p is false. So the second disjunct "goes without saying" for someone who asserts p. But the disjunction "p, or I am much mistaken" will be true *whether or not p is true.* It manages this by canvassing the possibility of being mistaken in advance. The disjunction will be *false* only in case p is false *and* I am *not* mistaken about p, in other words, if I do not believe that p. The form of words preserves truth in the face of the falsehood of what it asserts by disjoining assertion of p with recognition that if p fails, the speaker is mistaken. In this way "p, or I am much mistaken" and, with it, "I believe that p," which expresses the same recognition of the possibility of error, stand as counterinstances to the Assertion Principle. The so-called "Principle" is only a generally reliable and plausible statement, which fails in some logically tricky but intelligible cases. Expressions of belief that allude to the possibility of error in case p is false are among these special cases that contradict it. They may be true when p is false. They assert p, notwithstanding.

The third-person version, "p or he is much mistaken," is an intelligible and actually used ascription of belief that p. This form makes it clear that the ascriber does say that the believer is committed on the belief itself, for that is why the believer will be mistaken if not-p. But of course the ascriber will not be mistaken, for he does not assert that p when he ascribes belief that p to another in this fancy way or any other way. The pair

> The cat is on the mat, or I am much mistaken,

> The cat is on the mat, or Joe is much mistaken,

demonstrate univocal discourse about belief that yields assertion of the belief in the first-person and assertion about the believer in the third-person. But what do ascriptions of belief ascribe to believers?

3. Belief and knowledge compared

To answer this question we have to be careful never to abandon the semantic character of belief that is expressed in another truistic principle which has the advantage over the Assertion Principle in that it is also true.

> The Semantic Principle: If S believes that p, then S is right about p or S is wrong about p.

The Semantic Principle conveys the potential epistemic asset or liability of belief that p in a way that is neglected in formulations like these:

(A) If S believes that p, then S has an inner neural inscription of p in his brain.
(B) If S believes that p, then S is in a causally defined functional state.
(C) If S believes that p, then S is disposed to behavior b in circumstances c.

The conditionals (A), (B), and (C) may all be truths, for all that we have argued. They do not capture the semantic character of belief because none of them indicates that S is right or wrong about anything in virtue of believing that p.[2]

Emphasis on the Semantic Principle suggests comparison with the concept of knowledge. We all agree that for a subject S to know that p, p must be true. In fact, belief is much more like knowledge than philosophers have supposed. Belief exhibits the same kind of irreducible connectedness to the world outside the believer as knowledge, though the connection is somewhat different and more complex. This is overlooked for the obvious reason that the truth of p is *not* a condition for "S believes that p," as it is a condition for "S knows that p."

Since, unlike knowledge, a belief may be either true or false, philosophers have proceeded as though the holding of belief that p could consist of some reality in a believer characterizable without reference to the truth or falsehood of p. This idea fits the fact that S can say, "I believe that p," and this will be true whether p is true or not. In the case of knowledge we appreciate that the concept involves more than describable states of the knower because, before knowledge that p can be ascribed, the *outer* world has to be checked to see if p is true. Belief, in contrast, does not require this checking, since what is said of S in ascribing belief to him is true or false in itself, whatever the outcome of an investigation of p.

But the Semantic Principle reminds us that one cannot believe that p without being either right about p or wrong about p. One truth value or the other is required for belief that p, just as essentially as the value *true* is required for knowledge that p. The fact that the concept of belief does not require *a particular* truth value generates the mistaken impression that being a true belief or a false belief is not essential to being a belief. We have to be attentive to a moderately subtle distinction. To ascribe belief that p to S, we need not know *whether* S is right about p or S is wrong about p, but we do need to know *that* S is right about p or S is wrong about p. That the believer must be either right or wrong about p reveals an essential relation to the truth value of p in the concept of belief that p. This is just as unavoidable as the involvement of the truth of p in the concept of knowledge that p. To be right or wrong about p, the believer must be the one or the other. Given that S believes that p, being right requires that p be true, and being wrong requires that p be false. Both are fatal to the idea that a belief is an inner reality.

From "S knows that p" we can conclude that p is true. What can we conclude from the fact that believing that p is being right about p or wrong about p? We can only say that "p is true or p is false" follows from "S believes that p." This comparison appears to defeat the claim that the belief is like knowledge in the relevant sense. For the proposition "p is true or p is false" needs no premise save the doctrine of bivalence, and the entailment "p is true or p is false" cannot show anything interesting about a belief statement. But this line of thought really only shows that the involvement of the truth value of p in "S knows that p" is not well expressed by saying that "p is true" follows from "S knows that p." For consider "S knows that p or S knows that not-p." This may be true whether p is true or not. So like "S believes that p," the disjunctive statement "S knows that p or S knows that not-p" entails only "p is true or p is false," which does not need the premise, and does not illustrate the involvement of the truth of what is known in the concept of knowledge. In order to recover the understanding that fails to be expressed by drawing the conclusion "p is true or p is false," we have to emphasize that the disjunctive assertion "S knows that p or S knows that not-p" cannot be true unless one of the disjuncts is true. Whichever disjunct is true, a specific truth value for p is entailed. So whether it is p or not-p that S knows, knowing it involves a truth value for p. It is in just this sense that whichever it is (S is right about p or S is wrong about p), a truth value for p is required. Although we do not know which of the disjoined "states" to ascribe to S, we know that he must be in just one of them if the disjunction is to hold.

We have to expect a plausible objection to this emphasis on the disjunctive character of the concept of belief. Must we not say that if p is true, S is right about p, because he believes that p, and if p is false, he is wrong about p, for the very same reason? One thing ought to characterize S in either case. This is his inner state of belief that p. The presence of the belief explains why it is that the believer is right if p turns out to be true and wrong if p turns out to be false. Therefore, the belief cannot be identified with the disjunctive circumstance that it explains.

I will not repeat the exposition of incoherence that flows from the idea that his holding the belief is a matter of fact about the believer which is independent of the belief. The reader can generate the argument by considering ascriptions and expressions of belief under the hypothesis that having the belief that p is one thing about the believer which is as it is whether p is true or p is false. But we have still to discover what ascriptions of belief ascribe.

If we set aside the idea that there is some one thing that is found in, or true of, S, such as an inner state that constitutes his belief that p and therefore explains his being right or wrong, then we have to turn to the risk of being right or wrong itself. This prospect of being right along with the risk of error is the disjunctive state ascribed to S in saying "S believes that p." In other words, I do not argue that belief is an essentially disjunctive concept because beliefs have to be either correct or incorrect. Rather, since we have established that a categorically ascribable state, independent of the truth of p, is not feasible, the disjunctive interpretation expresses the essence of the concept of belief.

We can still understand the explanatory discourse that engenders this objection. Knowing that S believes that p explains his being right about p when we find that p is true, because before we know that p is true, we know only that S is either right or wrong. In the same way, believing that p explains that S is wrong about p, if we discover that p is false. Neither of these explanatory functions presupposes that believing that p is something like an inner state which is present or characterizes S in just the same way whether he is right or wrong. Belief that p can be *essentially* disjunctive, and explanatory discourse will be unaffected.

4. Belief on p, and belief that p

We said that the conditionals (A), (B), and (C) above (page 33) may be true. None of them convey the idea that a believer is either right or wrong about what he believes. Since they delete the essential semantic character of belief, we cannot hope to make any of these conditionals into biconditionals and then promote the right side of the biconditional to the status of an *identification of the state of belief that p* or an *analysis* of the truth conditions for "S believes that p." What about the Semantic Principle itself: If S believes that p, then S is right about p or S is wrong about p? We cannot make this into a biconditional either, and, therefore, as it stands, it is not a candidate for the analysis or identification of what it is to believe that p. In this case, however, the reason for which we cannot assert the converse, and thus the biconditional, is that the very same right side is equally appropriate for belief that not-p. Thus from the Semantic Principle we can conclude

(D_1): If S believes that p, S is right about p or S is wrong about p,

and equally,

(D_2): If S believes that not-p, then S is right about p or S is wrong about p.

Being right or wrong about p does express the semantic character of belief. It is simply a broader concept than that of belief that p. Furthermore, (D_1) and (D_2) do put us in a position to assert a biconditional that is a satisfactory philosophical understanding of the broader concept. Let us use the expression "has a belief *on* p" to mean "believes that p or believes that not-p." We can assert

(D_3): S has a belief on p, if, and only if, S is right about p or S is wrong about p.

(We can also speak of "knowledge on p" possessed by a subject who either knows that p or knows that not-p.) If we want to preserve the vocabulary of belief states, we can *identify* S's state of having a belief on p with the disjunctive state: Being right about p or being wrong about p. This "state" can be ascribed to S by another, or it can be self-ascribed by S. The ascription has the same force in either the first or the third person. It expresses the semantic character of belief in that it makes ineliminable reference to the world and is not an "inner" state or mere descriptive fact about S in any sense. It is disjunctive, so it does not ascribe anything to S categorically or without qualification.

There is no one thing ascribed to S whether he is right about p or wrong about p. S is in the disjunctive state if, and only if, S is in one or the other of the two nondisjunctive states that are disjoined. As we noted above, whichever of the nondisjunctive states S is in, assertion that S is in *that* state would require the assertion that p is true or that p is false.

The state of being right or wrong about p, identified with "having a belief on p," does not assert p itself when self-ascribed in the first person. That this self-ascription does not assert p is directly due to the fact that it is a broader concept than belief that p. Being in this state, S may believe that not-p or believe that p, and it is for that reason that it cannot be expected that assertion of p be part of the force of a first-person statement of belief on p. Now we want to go beyond this, and we want to find an ascription which has the same meaning in the first and the third person but which ascribes just belief that p and not the broader concept of belief on p. What we want will bring out the semantic character of belief just as being right or wrong about p does, and what we want is something which asserts that p when expressed in the first person.

Looking at the biconditional (D₃) from which the analysis of the broad concept of belief on p is derived, we can see that there are two factors, both of which have to be added to enable us to specify whether S is right about p or S is wrong about p. First we have to know whether it is p or not-p that S takes to be true, and, second, we have to know whether p is in fact true or p is in fact false. Thus, to move from "S is right about p or S is wrong about p" to a nondisjunctive claim requires information about the world (Is p true or false?) and information about S (Is it p or not-p that S endorses?). Intuitively it seems as though it is only the latter information about S that we need in order to reach an analysis of "believes that p." Surely we do not have to know whether p is itself true in order to know that S believes that p, although we do have to know whether p is true or false in order to know whether S is right in believing that p. But we have seen that the effort to identify belief that p with the help of information restricted to facts about the believer cannot succeed. For such facts could always be stated by the believer without asserting that p.

At the same time we are confronted with the thought that the additional information about the world, namely, the information that p is true, or that p is false, *does not* advance our understanding of

S when we already know that S is right about p or wrong about p. Knowing, for example, that p is true is not helpful since it may be not-p that S believes. It is as though, knowing everything relevant that we can know about the outside world, we still cannot discriminate belief that p from belief that not-p, so it appears that we must look to things about S for the discriminating factor.

In a sense this is true, but it is not a sense that rehabilitates an inner-state interpretation. Of course, we need information about S and not information about the world. We have never denied that the ascription of belief "S believes that p" expresses something knowable about S and does not assert p. But the information we need about S should have the special feature that it is not information about S from S's point of view. From his point of view the very thing we say about him must turn into an assertion of p when S says it himself. We need information which is at the same time information about S for others and a claim about the world for S himself.

5. The rôle of the risk of being mistaken

The rhetorical expression of belief "p or I am much mistaken" to which we drew attention in refuting the Assertion Principle permits the inelegant reformulation

(1) If p is false, then I am wrong about p.

And since "p or I am much mistaken" expresses commitment to the truth of p, it also carries the force

(2) If p is true, then I am right about p.

Combining (1) and (2) we have

(3) If p is true, then I am right about p; and if p is false, then I am wrong about p.

Generally, two conditionals jointly asserted yield no categorical conclusion. For example, from

If interest rates rise, I will sell my government bonds; and if the dollar weakens, I will buy common stocks of major exporters, it does not follow that I will do either, since both antecedents may fail. But because p has to be either true or false, from the joint assertion of the two conditionals in (3) the disjunction "I am right about p or I am wrong about p" can be drawn. As we have said, this disjunction asserts that one or the other of the disjuncts is true. Each disjunct requires a truth value for p, so that neither could be identified with an inner state. But the disjunction here is the one that we have already identified with holding a belief *on* p, so we have made no apparent progress.

There has been a loss of content, however, since (3) expresses belief that p and not merely belief on p. The content is restored if we transform (3) into the logically equivalent form:

(4) If p is true, then p is true and I am right about p; and if p is false, then p is false and I am wrong about p.

which with "p is true or p is false" entails

(5) Either p is true and I am right about p, or p is false and I am wrong about p.

(5) indicates that it is the state of belief that p, rather than not-p, that I have. It succeeds in the desired narrowing of the broader concept of having a belief *on* p, although it appeals only to the concept of being right or wrong about p, and the possible truth values of p. It does not include further information about the believer. Thus (5) continues to exploit the semantic character of belief which requires determinations about the world in individuation of the believer's "state." Restating (5) as a biconditional about any believer S, we reach the desired analysis: "S believes that p," if, and only if,

(6) p is true and S is right about p, or p is false and S is wrong about p.

The disjunction (6) is like "S knows that p, or S knows that not-p" in its reliance on a truth value for p. The truth of the disjunction requires one or the other of the nondisjunctive propositions: "p is true and S is right about p" or "p is false and S is wrong about p," each of which contains a particular truth value for p.

If we look at just the first disjunct, we find that it conjoins the two categorical claims: first, "p is true," and, second, "I am right about p." The second disjunct has a parallel structure. The analysis of belief

I have reached here claims that belief involves the truth value of what is believed, just as knowledge involves the truth of what is known. The structure of (6) makes it appear that the justification of the claim that belief is like knowledge stems from the fact that each disjunct here contains the categorical specification of a truth value for p. Of course, one disjunct does contain "p is true" and the other "p is false." *But the claim that belief is like knowledge is not based on this.* The requirement of one or the other of the truth values for p is already imposed by "I am right about p, or I am wrong about p," for each of these disjuncts requires a truth value for p. The introduction of "p is true" and "p is false" in the disjuncts composing (6) is not motivated by a need to bring in a truth value for p. It only serves the purpose of distinguishing between belief *that p* and belief *that not-p*. It succeeds by specifying which truth value appears in which disjunct. That one or the other does is established already. I have approached the concept of "belief that p" through "belief on p" partly in order to establish that the broader concept by itself manifests the dependence of the concept of belief on a truth value for p, as we noted in discussion of the state of being right or being wrong about p.

We have reconstructed the desired concept of belief that p without recourse to information about S, which seems necessary whenever our perspective gravitates back to the inner-state outlook. As an explication of "belief that p," (6) automatically satisfies the requirements of both the first and the third person. We have shown that the first-person version, (5), does assert p, since it is a transformation of "p, or I am much mistaken." But the third-person version, "Either p is true and Joe is right about p, or p is false and Joe is wrong about p," does not assert that p. (6) conveys information that can be learned about Joe by others who do not thereby learn that p. This is not mysterious. It simply reflects the fact that it is the one who believes that p and not someone who ascribes that belief to him that stands to be right or wrong about p. Therefore, if we think of the disjunction as a "state" of S, an ascription of the state characterized in (6) conveys the idea that S believes that p, while it does not assert that p. The first-person version of the same statement is an assertion of p. It is the assertion "p, or I am much mistaken."

We might add a final observation on the disjunctive character of the analysis of "believes that p" that is articulated in (6). The fact that an ascription of belief does not assert the belief while an expression of belief does is made graspable here. Someone ascribing belief that p to Joe can rest satisfied with the disjunctive status of (6). He does not make any claim as to which of the disjuncts it is that secures the applicability of the disjunction. It is simply one of them or the other. Either p is true and Joe is right, or p is false and Joe is wrong. The ascriber can remain neutral. But Joe's perspective *has to be* something entirely different. Joe cannot say, "It is just that p is true and I am right, or p is false and I am wrong," and adopt a skeptical neutrality as to whether he is right or he is wrong. The reason for this has nothing to do with an inner state or any other *one thing* that Joe has whether p is true or false. It is rather the fact that asserting (3) (which is the first-person version of (6)) is asserting p. Joe would not be right or wrong were he not asserting that p is true, which the ascriber is not doing at all. Joe cannot assert

> I am not saying that p is true. I just want to let you know
> that I am right in case p is true or wrong in case it isn't.

How could he possibly be right if p is true and wrong if p is false if he is not saying that p is true? Of course, the answer is that he could not.

6. What is true of those who believe

In spite of everything we have argued, all the force of the traditional ways of thinking about belief and the inner life are likely to press themselves on us again with an appeal that seems irresistible.

"S believes that p" makes a statement about S. We have said that this means that S is right about p and p is true, or S is wrong about p and p is false. But we still face the question "In virtue of what is S right about p given that p is true?" It is not because p is true that S is right about it. But this just drives us back to the thought that S's believing that p must be something about S specifiable independently of the issue of the truth or falsehood of p, such that, given this something about S, he is right if p, and wrong if not-p.

We have urged a disjunctive understanding of belief that p. Believing *is* being right or wrong. But doesn't this merely create an atmosphere of mysteriousness? It is as though we make S's being right or being wrong brute and unanalyzable by disallowing that his belief that p can have any constitution in S that could be described without assigning any truth value to p. But how do we find out whether S is right or wrong? We find what S believes, and then we check to see whether *that* is true. We could not very well just find out whether or not p is right or wrong without *independently* finding out what it is that S believes. If we could not independently determine that S believes that p, without raising the question of p at all, then determining the truth value of p would have no relevance to the question of S being right or wrong.

Here we are being baffled by the difference in the perspective of the believer and of the perspective of others. Of course, when someone else wants to decide whether or not S is right about p, that inquirer has to know what S's stand is, and this has to be something independent of the truth of p. It is correct to say that if this inquirer could not specify S's belief without saying anything about the truth value of p, discourse about belief that p could not get off the ground at all.

At this point we ought to be able to say something about S that is not disjunctive but categorical in ascribing belief to S, something that is only about S. Then we can go on to consider the truth value of p. But this way of thinking is surely a preparation for the introduction of something like an inner-belief state. We know how S represents things in his mind, and then we check things to see if they are as S represents them.

What is the believer's perspective? Let us say S wonders about p. Of course, while he is wondering about p, he is not trying to decide whether he believes that p or not. By hypothesis he does not. He is trying to decide whether to believe p or not. And that is just the same as trying to decide whether p or not. As soon as he decides that p is true, he believes that p. There is no job for an inner representation from this point of view. Of course, we can say, "He represents it that p." But from S's point of view there is no such thing as an independent fact that he believes that p which has to be specifiable before the truth or falsehood of p can be relevant to his being right or wrong. "Representation" is just a synonym for "belief" here, not a key element in the process of believing.

From the perspective of the believer the atmosphere of troubling paradox about the bruteness of being right or wrong about p disappears. Our thought was that we must be able to specify that S believes that p independently of determining a truth value for p in order to make the truth value of p relevant to the question of S's being right or being wrong. Like others, S knows that he is right in the belief that p if p is true, and wrong if p is false. He knows that he may be the one or the other. But S cannot say,

> I must specify my belief that p independently of determining a truth value for p, for otherwise a truth value for p will have no relevance to my being right or wrong. I have to be able to say something like: "Here is my representation, and it agrees or disagrees with the world."

In one sense "S believes that p" says something about S in that it says that S is right or wrong about p. This is an empirical fact, independent of p itself, in that S might have no opinion on p or might believe that not-p. The disjunction accommodates very comfortably the truth-value independence of ascriptions and expressions from the beliefs they ascribe and express. Both ascriptions and expressions of belief are insulated from overthrow by one or the other truth value of p, because in making a disjunctive claim both allow for either eventuality from the outset.

7. Conclusion

The analysis of belief given here has significant implications. The concept of belief has been explicated without appeal to inner goings-on of any sort, whether physical or nonphysical. The extent to which concepts other than belief can be understood in an analogous, ontologically conservative fashion has to be investigated. In the opinion of this writer such analysis of the focal concepts of perceptual experience and desire can be carried out successfully. There is less to "the mind" than we philosophers have supposed. The analysis excludes all identity theories together, insofar as these theories are supposed to account for the character of belief. It also excludes behaviorist analysis, which, like the identity theories, offers an account of expressions of belief that construes them as autobiographical statements, although not claims about inner states. In agreement with identity theory to this extent, behaviorism fails to represent expressions of belief as assertions of what is believed. Perhaps most far-reaching is the implied repudiation of the causal reading of reason-giving explanations which adduce beliefs and desires in explanation of actions. If appeal to beliefs is not appeal to any reality at all in the believer, then it is not appeal to a causal factor in the believer. I will return to this theme in chapter 7.

NOTES

1. See J. L. Austin, "Performative Utterances," *Philosophical Papers*, Oxford, 1961. For the affinity of "I know" and "I promise" see J. L. Austin, "Other Minds," *Proceedings of the Aristotelian Society*, Supplementary vol. XX, 1946; reprinted in *Philosophical Papers*, esp. pp. 98-103.

2. The expressions "right about p" and "wrong about p" are not technical, but to be clear we may explain them thus:

(a) "S is right about p" is true, iff, S believes that p, and p is
true; or S believes that not-p, and p is false,

and

(b) "S is wrong about p" is true, iff, S believes that p, and p is
false; or S believes that not-p, and p is true.

Being right or wrong about p are not exhaustive alternatives like the alternatives, p is true or p is false. If S has no view about p, he is neither right nor wrong about p. The three element disjunction:

(c) "S is right about p, or S is wrong about p, or S has no opinion about p," is exhaustive.

From (c) it follows that S is right about p or S is wrong about p, if S has any opinion on p, and the Semantic Principle is an immediate consequence.

III

Pointing Models for Discourse about Belief

1. Theories about belief and truth conditions for ascriptions

It is one thing for S to believe that p is true and another thing for p to be true. This obvious distinction is especially prominent in ascriptions of belief. Plainly, we do not say that there is life on Mars when we say, "Joe believes that there is life on Mars." Philosophical theories about belief all try to be specific about what it is for someone to believe that p. They do not let it go by saying that holding the belief is one thing and the truth of the belief is something else. They say what that *one thing* is. The truth of an ascription is independent of the truth of the belief. The theories try to say just what it is that an ascription ascribes to a believer. They say that the underlying reality of belief is a behavioral disposition, or a brain state, or a functional state, or a spiritual state of the believer.

The relationship between various theories of belief and the idea of the independence of ascriptions of belief and beliefs ascribed is summarized in the following Table:

TRUTH CONDITIONS

Column A	Column B
(ascription of belief)	*(belief ascribed)*
Theory (1): Joe has disposition D.	Life on Mars.
Theory (2): Joe has brain state B.	Life on Mars.
Theory (3): Joe has functional state F.	Life on Mars.
Theory (4): Joe has ethereal state E.	Life on Mars.
Theory (5): Joe has ?	Life on Mars.

The theories all exploit the independence of the column A matter of fact and the column B matter of fact in a straightforward way. Each theory provides an explicit subject matter other than p to be the subject matter of the ascription. I include the blank theory (5) to emphasize reliance on the idea of independence here. If the articulated theories (1) through (4) all failed, we would have to find a new characterization of the truth condition for the ascription. Something else about Joe would have to constitute his holding the belief that there is life on Mars. For there must be a truth condition for the column A matter of fact.

The trouble with all the philosophical theories of belief is now easily stated. All the theories, including the prospective theory (5), provide an explicit subject matter for ascriptions of belief. Each theory makes it clear just what fact is ascribed to Joe in saying that he holds the belief that p. The truth condition for the ascription in each case is just an ascertainable fact about Joe. It is indisputable that the believer could state these facts himself. Joe could make assertions that have the force "The truth conditions for the ascription of belief that p obtain in my case." Joe can make assertions about Joe's dispositions, about the functional rôles played by his own states, about what is in Joe's own brain, or in his immortal soul. He might be wrong about any of these matters. The fact that he speaks of his own dispositions or states, of whatever variety, does not guarantee that what he says will always be correct. The point is that he can meaningfully make these assertions about himself. This is perfectly obvious and incontestable. In other words, given these theories, we are entitled to translate the items of column A into first-person statements. Joe can say, "I have such and such a disposition" or "My brain is manifesting such and such." In each case Joe will be saying, within the framework of one of the theories, "the conditions for ascription of belief that p to me are satisfied." In short, he would be saying that he believes that p. These first-person formulations would be self-ascriptions of belief. The theories themselves guarantee this. The whole point of the theories is to identify his holding a belief with some fact about Joe. The theories stem from, and utterly rely upon, the difference between the fact about Joe and the fact about Mars formulated in p itself.

I want to stress that calling attention to the first-person case is not based on a doubtful or mischievous extension of the intent of theories like those summarized in the table. No philosopher identifying belief in the spirit of one of these theories supposes that everyday reports of beliefs are understood by ordinary speakers to be reports on their own dispositions or brain-states. The idea is that we are all able to report our belief-states in ordinary language without having any idea of just what it is that constitutes those states. Philosophers of mind promoting one or another of these theories sometimes emphasize they are not explicating the meaning of belief statements. They do not restate what an ordinary speaker conveys in reporting his belief. Nonetheless, the theories themselves purport to tell us about the constitution of the very states that are reported in ordinary terms by ordinary speakers. Once the true nature of the state of belief that p is successfully identified by philosophers or scientists, a believer will (in principle) be able to report the presence of his own belief states characterized as the theory characterizes them.

If he should come to know the nature of his own belief-state, Joe will not conflate assertions having the column A truth condition with assertions having the column B truth condition. He cannot be so muddled or stupid as to think that the assertion that he has a certain disposition or a certain brain state is somehow a claim to the effect that Mars has living things on it. He appreciates the utter independence of these matters just as anyone else does. Then, when he says of himself, "I have this disposition" or "I have this brain state," he will not be saying that there is life on Mars or expressing any stand on that issue. That will be a different matter altogether for him. He may be committed to the truth of p. But in making an assertion with truth conditions from column A, he will not be saying whether he is committed to the truth of "There is life on Mars," which quite conspicuously has the column B truth condition. He will merely self-ascribe belief that p and will take no stand on p itself, just as another who makes a column A assertion about Joe takes no stand on the satisfaction of the column B condition.

But, as we noted in chapter 2, a man cannot intelligibly say that he holds a belief and leave unaddressed the question of the truth of the belief he says he holds. To say that he himself believes that p is precisely to express the stand he takes on p, namely, that it is true. If any of the theories of belief were correct, Joe would able to say that the conditions for ascription of belief that p to him are met without committing himself on the truth of p at all. That is incoherent, so none of the theories is correct.

The double question of truth—Does the subject believe that p? and Is it the case that p?—in the context of ascriptions and expressions of belief is the locus of the failure of mind-brain identity and dualist identity theories of belief. It is also the locus of the difficulties illustrated by Moore's paradox, and it is what makes the transformation of neutral ascriptions of belief to first-person assertions of the belief puzzling. In order to shed light on all of these matters, I will describe imaginary alternatives to the natural linguistic devices that we use in communicating with one another about our beliefs. Since they will not involve speaking, these schemes for ascription and expression of belief handle the double question of truth in unfamiliar ways. As a consequence the models throw into relief features of ascription and expression that are hard to notice in our ordinary unproblematic way of speaking.

2. A behavioristic pointing model

Imagine a society of people who resemble us in most ways, and in particular in that they have beliefs much like our beliefs. The members of this society have the use of language, but they can neither speak nor write. Remarkably enough, they can read. By some natural process each man comes to possess a list of sentences that has on it the things he might want to assert. Unable to make an intelligible sound or to create an inscription of a sentence, these people point to sentences on their lists and thereby accomplish what we do when we make assertions. Generally, as we have said, assertion of p is the commonest means of expression of belief that p. In the imagined society, pointing to a sentence expresses a belief. Sally and Joe are citizens of this society.

It might turn out that Joe's list has on it sentences such as these:

p: There is life on Mars.
q_1: Sally pointed to p.
q_2: Sally frequently points to p.
q_3: Sally now points to p.

Pointing has the force of commitment to the truth of what is pointed to. Pointing does not assert more than the sentence pointed to. That a person pointed to a sentence, or frequently points to a sentence, or is presently doing so are all things that can be asserted by pointing to sentences like those which we have excerpted from Joe's list. It is easy to imagine that many common conversational functions of speech will be manageable in this society when people point to their lists in the presence of others and for the benefit of others.

The interesting feature of this model is just this: The sentence to which a man can point and thereby let it be known that he is committed to the truth of p is the sentence p itself.* But a "pointer" in this society cannot convey information about his own commitment to a sentence on his list by pointing to sentences about his own pointings. Of course, a man's list can have on it sentences about his own pointings and thus about his own commitments. For example, the following sentences could appear on Joe's list, could be true, and could properly be asserted by pointing to them:

r_1: I pointed to p.
r_2: I frequently point to p.

The sentence r_1, like q_1, plainly does not express commitment to p, although by pointing to it Joe can assert that he did express commitment to p in the past. Pointing to r_1 is like the first-person past-tense belief statement in that it is compatible with the denial that the belief is true. The sentences r_2 and q_2 are alike in that pointing to them will ascribe a behavioral disposition to a person, a disposition that would naturally be manifested by someone committed to the truth of p. But ascription of this disposition, in either the first person or the third person, is patently not itself an assertion that there is life on Mars, and is compatible with asserting (pointing to) the denial of this statement.[1] Now let us imagine that Joe's list might have on it the further sentence

r_3: I now point to p,

which would be a first-person parallel for q_3.

How should we interpret Joe's pointing to this sentence? To understand this question we want to imagine ourselves members of this society, so as to taste the first-person point of view as they experience it. It seems that by pointing to r_3 on my list I could assert something about my present commitment to p, just as I can assert something about Sally's present commitment to p by pointing to q_3, and just as I can assert something about my own past commitment to p by pointing to r_1. However, although I could assert r_3 by pointing to it (if it is on my list), it seems that I could never assert anything true by pointing

---

*We will also expect that commitment to p could be manifested by pointing to other sentences which entail p when it could be reasonably surmised that this entailment would be recognized by any witness to the pointing.

to r_3! For r_3 says that I point to p, which I do not since r_3 is not p. The inevitable failure of pointing to r_3 as a way of expressing my commitment to p is like the failure of attempts to say that I believe that p without asserting p itself.

We may feel that the unavoidable falsehood of my assertion in pointing to r_3 is only a technicality or a quibble. Could we not eliminate the difficulty, or the appearance of a difficulty, by imagining that these believers can point to more than one sentence at a time, or by including on my list conjunctions such as

p&r_3: p and I now point to p.

Such devices would represent in the model the idea that "I believe that p" might have a compound force, asserting that p and also asserting the separable claim that I hold that belief, that the belief-state is present. It is in order, and in keeping with our customary thinking about conjunction, to say that a man can be right in committing himself to a conjunction only if he would be right in committing himself to each of the conjuncts separately. "p and Sally points to p" satisfies this ruling, but "p and I point to p" does not. Similarly, it seems reasonable to require that a man can be right in simultaneous pointings only if he would be right in pointing to each of the sentences by itself. Simultaneous selection of p and q_3 conforms to this rule, but simultaneous selection of p and r_3 violates it.

Even if we waive these very plausible rules, pointing to conjunctions or to more than one sentence at a time does not yield a vehicle by which a man could make a true assertion that is *only* about his commitment to the truth of a sentence. For no sentence X can I point only to "I point to X" and be right about anything, unless I also point simultaneously to X itself, or unless X itself is also a conjunct in a conjunction to which I point. This corresponds to the fact that I cannot say only that I hold a belief without asserting that belief. In ascribing a belief to another I can point merely to "Sally points to p," and I will be right if Sally is pointing to p. But I cannot point only to "I point to p" and be right about something. I cannot correctly ascribe a belief to myself without asserting it. The very idea of self-ascription of belief that can be detached from assertion of the belief is an illusion supported by a natural but incorrect interpretation of ascriptions and expressions of belief. The illusion comes from the double issue of truth.

The double issue of truth is represented in the model in the following way: Pointing to p, I assert that p, and I will be wrong if p is false. Others will rightly gather from my pointing to p that I stand to be wrong if p is false, that I am committed to the truth of p, in short, that I believe that p. If they point to the sentence "AC points to p," they will assert something true about me. This is like an ascription of belief to me. But my expression of the belief that p does not assert what another's ascription of belief that p to me asserts. In my expression of belief that p by pointing to p I do not assert that I point to p; I assert only p. An ascription of belief, by pointing to "AC points to p," does assert that I, AC, believe that p but does not assert p. Here we find, under the pointing convention for expressing belief, a curious metamorphosis in the transition from the third- to the first-person procedure for conveying the information that AC believes that p. If I want to point to something that will authorize your ascription of belief that p to me, I have to point to p. If I merely point to sentences about myself and my states, I will not get anything asserted about Mars, and you will not know that I stand to be wrong in case there is no life on Mars. You will have no reason for thinking that I am committed to the truth of that proposition. You will have no ground for ascribing to me belief that there is life on Mars. The defect of pointing to "I point to p" makes this clear, since the assertion I make in that pointing will be conspicuously false whether or not there is life on Mars.

The potential for confusion in our own verbal procedures for ascribing and expressing belief is visible in the relationship of the expression and ascription of belief that p to the general proposition "Someone believes that p." This proposition follows from what is asserted in pointing to "Sally points to p." In contrast, "Someone points to p" does not follow from what is asserted in pointing to p, for only p is asserted. However, *it follows* that someone points to p, if I do, and others can rightly ascribe belief that p to me if I express belief that p. When they do so, they will not be reasserting in the third person anything that I asserted, since I asserted only p. Finally, if I do point to p, and p turns out to be false, I can then point to r_1, "I pointed to p," and that will be true, but it will not be a reassertion of anything I asserted earlier when I expressed the belief that p.

These relationships exhibited in the pointing model for discourse are also manifested in our actual verbal techniques for ascription and expression of belief. If I express the belief that p by asserting that p, that someone believes that p does not follow from what I assert. But my expression of the belief will suffice to justify another's ascription, "AC believes that p," to me, and "Someone believes that p" does follow, as the existential generalization of the ascription of belief that p.

Surprisingly, we have to say that "Someone believes that p" does not follow from "I believe that p," even though it follows that someone believes that p, if I do. "Someone believes that p" would follow from this verbal formulation for expression of belief only if we could legitimately regard it as a self-ascription. But we have seen in chapter 2 that this is not possible. Since the assertion "I believe that p" is a weakened form of the assertion that p, it is an assertion of p. Therefore, existential generalization does not apply since the assertion does not register me in the class of believers that p but says that p is true. Therefore, it is not correct to suppose that "Someone believes that p" is entailed by what I say when I say, "I believe that p."

Furthermore, as in the world of pointing discourse, so in our own actual world, if p proves false when I have expressed the belief that p, I can say, "I believed that p," and this will be true. It will not reassert what I asserted earlier when I expressed the belief that p, for then I only asserted p, and that is what has turned out to be false.

The phrase "I believe that" actually functions to express the relative insecurity of the speaker concerning p, as we said above. The occurrence of the phrase does not introduce a distinct subject matter or make a further claim, as compared with the unqualified assertion that p. Within the pointing model distinctions in confidence concerning p might be marked by differences in gesture: perhaps a sliding scale from very hesitant to very bold pointings, or pointing with the thumb to moral certainties, and to propositions of logic and mathematics; with the index finger to reasonably certain matters of fact; while reserving the pinky for pointing to beliefs that are hardly more than hunches.

Why should we include distinctions in degree of confidence in the pointing gesture rather than in separate sentences on lists, sentences such as "I am morally certain that p" and "I have a hunch that p"? This seems to be the correct handling of relative certainty because it is just the truth or falsehood of p that will determine whether I am right or wrong, if my belief is very confident, or if it is just a hunch. Thus, although it includes a mark of relative insecurity, "I believe that p" asserts only p and does not make a separate assertion to the effect that the speaker is uncertain. In consequence, though it sounds odd, it is proper to say "I believed that p" and "He believes that p" are not restatements of "I believe that p" in the past tense and in the third person, respectively. For the first two statements are not assertions of p, while the last is.

Attention to this same point should also make us comfortable in the claim that "Someone believed that p" does not follow from what is asserted in saying, "I believe that p." Although others will rightly gather that someone believes that p when I have said, "I believe that p," what I have asserted, with notice of my uncertainty in asserting it, is merely p. That someone points to p does not follow from what I point to when I point to p, whether I point with thumb or pinky.

3. A materialist pointing model

The imaginary practice that we have considered so far manages both ascription and expression of belief by pointing to sentences. Sentences on lists to which these believers point do not include "Sally believes that p" or "I believe that p," since the work of these sentences has been transferred to the activity of pointing. Omitting any sentences containing "believes" from lists of sentences that may be pointed to has the effect of reducing the concept of having a belief to the concept of expressing a belief. Within the resources of the model, all ascriptions of belief must assert that someone *expresses* a belief, that is, points to a sentence. In this respect, if we included conditionals specifying circumstances under which pointing is manifested, the pointing model would be a simple picture of a behaviorist conception of belief.

The reduction of holding a belief to expressing a belief is a weakness in the model. That Sally holds the belief that p explains assertions of p and explains her disposition to assert that p in various circumstances. This explanation is lost by the behaviorist version of the pointing model, as it is in all behaviorist accounts of belief. The fault does not invalidate the use of the model to help us to resist temptations to misconstrue the force of "I believe that p" in our actual discourse about belief. But we can construct a slightly different pointing model that is able to represent assertions about possession of belief that do not collapse into assertions about expressions of belief. For this purpose we can retain intact the pointing practices of the first model and change only our conception of the lists of sentences.

Now we will have to think of each person's list as somehow attached to that person as a biological part. The visible markings of butterflies, birds, and fish do play a primitive role in communication between animals, so we might imagine that lists of sentences represent an extreme evolutionary development of "markings." Each person's list does not contain all the sentences which could possibly figure in ascriptions of belief, that is, all the things a person might believe. We will imagine that each list is comprised of all and only the sentences that formulate beliefs of the person whose list it is. Since beliefs change over time, we can imagine that the sentences on a person's list change by some physiological process of erasure and inscription.

Finally we suppose that this attached list of beliefs is perceivable by others and legible to them. This is required if others are to make sense of the pointing performances of a believer. It follows that others could ascertain whether or not a man believes that p by reading his list, even if he does not call attention to his belief by pointing to it on his list. This, of course, is not a defect in the model as compared to our actual practices. As these matters are managed in fact, we can often discover that men hold the beliefs that they do without relying entirely on their expressions of belief. At worst the model makes this possibility more prominent and more general.

A minor defect which does not affect our use of the model is that under the conditions it envisions it would be impossible for a man to misrepresent his belief by asserting something that he does not believe. A society whose discourse conformed to this model could dispense with oaths given in court prior to testimony, and the circumstances of the model would make police interrogation all too easy. This is so because, by hypothesis, a man's visible and legible list would contain all of and only his beliefs.

In addition to sentences like p, q_1, q_2, q_3, r_1, and r_2 that we have found unproblematic in the first model, we can now have sentences that make assertions about the constituents of lists that comprise an individual's beliefs. There will be sentences such as these:

s: p is on Sally's list.
t: p is on my list.

Unlike q_3 of the first model, the sentence s is true if Sally believes that p, whether or not she ever expresses that belief. So s is a better representation of an ascription of belief than anything available in the first model. If self-ascription of belief were feasible at all, the sentence t might be expected to capture the force of a self-ascription where r_3, "I now point to p," failed. The failure of r_3 might appear to be a consequence of the fact that it really self-ascribes expression of belief and not possession of belief. The sentence t makes a claim about the standing composition of my list and not about my episodic pointing behavior. As such it will not run into the particular difficulties r_3 encountered.

We said that the first pointing model is behaviorist in spirit because it reduces the idea of possession of belief to the idea of overt pointing actions and dispositions to such actions. The emended pointing model suggests materialist philosophy of mind which would be articulated by an identity theory expressed as

S believes that p = p is on S's list.

In virtue of the claim this identity theory makes, to point to, and thus to assert, the sentence t: "p is on my list" is to assert that I believe that p. t is a self-ascription of belief that has the same neutrality about the truth of p as the ordinary ascription "p is on AC's list." What t asserts can be true whether or not p is true, for it only asserts that p is on my list, and this will be true, if p *is* on my list. Thus, the identity theory here expresses the natural but misleading thought that a man saying, "I believe that p" is asserting something that will be true as long as he does believe that p, whether or not p itself is true.

The envisioned identity theory within the terms of this second pointing model is close in spirit to versions of materialism that are presently entertained and espoused. All those identity theories that speak of neural encodings, of inscriptions stored in the brain, or of *neuralese*, the language of brain encodings, envision an identity for belief-states that has the logical force of identifying a belief-state with a sentence on a certain list. We might say that, relative to these currently defended versions of materialist identity, our model identity theory differs mostly by putting inscriptions of sentences on external rather than internal tissues, and by presenting English as the language of the physical reality of belief-states. The minimal plausibility of the identity theory ought not to hinge on the inscriptions being tucked away in inaccessible corners of the cortex, nor should the logical force of "sentential-state" theory[2] be impaired by making the language of the inscriptions easy to decipher.

It may be noted at once that the identification of belief-states with sentences on physiological lists, which our model theory and all other inscription theories propose, does not generate any curious metamorphosis from p-neutral ascriptions of belief in the third person to assertions of p when the belief is expressed by the person to whom it is properly ascribed. "My list has p on it" does not assert p anymore than does "AC's list has p on it." Thus, in the spirit of all identity theories the imaginary model makes it possible for a believer to say that a belief-state is present in him without asserting that that belief is true. If we make this metamorphosis a criterion for successful characterization of belief-states, we should expect to find that the model identification theory is inadequate. The pattern of reasoning here would defeat any sentential-state identification of beliefs.

There is nothing incoherent about the sentence "p is on my list" within the framework of the assumptions of the model. Its truth conditions are obvious. In the first pointing model we saw that an effort at self-ascription made by pointing to "I point to p" failed because no true assertion could be made by pointing to this sentence. In the emended model I can point to "p is on my list" and assert something true. I will be asserting that p is on my list, and what I assert will be true if p is, indeed, on my list. Why could pointing to t not be a means for self-ascribing belief that p within the resources of the pointing model?

Perhaps the rhythm of the dialectic that generates the answer to this question has become familiar to the reader. If this were a self-ascription, I would be able to say that I believe that p without taking any stand at all on the truth of p. What stand I take on p, if any, is simply something else that my list will show, under the hypothesis of the model. If "p is on my list" is itself a sentence on my list, I can assert it by pointing to it, but I do not get p asserted in that way. I may not be able to get p asserted at all, for I will not be able to assert p if p is not on my list, even though "p is on my list" is on my list.

By hypothesis all of my beliefs are on my list. So the presence of "p is on my list" means that I believe that p is on my list and that I am committed to the truth of that proposition. But the presence of "p is on my list" does not resolve, even for me, the question of my commitment to the truth of p itself. Its presence only shows that I am committed to something about my list of sentences. It shows that *that* proposition about my list is one of my beliefs. But p itself is the proposition "There is life on Mars," which has nothing to do with my list.

Another man directly reading my list of beliefs and finding "p is on my list" on it will not thereby know whether or not I believe that p. For that he must find p itself on my list. But then, if I draw another's attention to "p is on my list" by pointing to it on my list, and thus asserting it, I call his attention to a sentence that does not let him know whether or not p is on my list. Thus, I do not let him know whether or not I believe that p. I would let him know at once that I do believe that p if, by pointing to p on my list, and thus asserting that p, I draw attention to the fact that I believe it since it is there on the list of all of my beliefs.

We have already encountered these defects in materialist identity theories before. The materialist always tries to identify my belief-state with some fact about myself that I could state in an autobiographical report. But this item of autobiography will not express my stand on the belief in question. As a consequence the information that this fact obtains in my case, whatever the fact is, will not authorize others to ascribe belief that p to me. To give others that authorization I have to assert that p, and no autobiographical report will succeed in doing that.

Ascriptions of belief to AC are all made by pointing to sentences about AC's list of sentences. But my expressions of belief will not refer to my list unless the belief I express happens to be a belief about my list.

A man could have a list of all of his beliefs. At least we have shown nothing against this. In point of fact the very notion of "all of a man's beliefs" is vexed, but it is vexed in ways that are irrelevant to our concerns.[3] So we will suppose that a man could have a list of all of his beliefs in his brain, or in his diary, or in exceedingly fine script on his forearm. The identity claim—to believe that p is to have p on one's list—could not possibly be true. Were it true, "p is on my list" would have to mean that I believe that p, because that is exactly what the identity theory contends. But "p is on my list" can be true and can be asserted by me without my taking any stand on p, and even though I believe that not-p, and even though not-p is on my list. It is incoherent to say that I believe that p and do not take any stand on p. So this identity theory cannot be correct.

In sum, the pointing models help to make intuitively clear the following ideas concerning belief and our natural discourse about belief: (1) Expressions of belief that p assert p. (2) A believer cannot assert that he holds the belief that p without asserting p. (3) Identity theories provide a subject matter for a believer which would enable him to assert that he holds the belief that p without asserting p. The pointing models indicate that this defect defeats all identity theories.

NOTES

1. This model has no way of distinguishing believing that p and expressing belief that p in the pointing action, or at least being disposed to the right pointing action. So the falsehood of "I point to p" has to cover the ground of both expressing belief that p (that is, asserting that p) and believing that p. The falsehood of "I point to p" is a consequence of the fact that the pointer does not assert p (point to p), which is what "I point to p" claims that he does do. This much does correspond to the failure of efforts at self-ascription of belief in our ordinary verbal practice. Like such self-ascriptions, pointing to "I point to p" fails because it does not assert that p. The coarseness of the model leaves open the possibility that the pointer does nonetheless believe that p. The inadequacies of the analysis that stem from this circumstance are well treated in the materialist model to be discussed below.

2. For a general critique of sentential-state and inner-inscription theories about belief see A. Collins, "Could Our Beliefs Be Representations in Our Brains?" *J.Phil.*, LXXVI, 5, 1979.

3. For example, are the infinite grammatical and logical transformations of p to be separate entries on the list of one who believes that p? If S believes that the moon is more than a mile from the earth, does S believe that the moon is more than one-half of a mile from the earth, one-quarter of a mile, one-eighth of a mile, . . . ? The idea of a list of all of S's beliefs raises the question of the individuation of beliefs and of the possible infinite length of such a list.

IV

The Concept of Consciousness

1. Some reflections on dualism

There are philosophical theories about consciousness and the nature of conscious phenomena. Perhaps "theories" is too definite an idea for philosophical thinking on this topic. I would say that mind-body dualism is a theory about consciousness apart from the fact that it offers so very little in the way of explanation of anything. In Descartes' view the idea that the mind is a nonmaterial constituent of a human being is largely a negative conception. Although his motivation is not very clearly reflected in the *Meditations*, through which his metaphysical views are best known today, Descartes rejects a physical conception of mental reality primarily because of his appreciation of the damage that psychologistic, teleological, and animistic thinking does in physical science.[1] It is no exaggeration to say that dualism is Descartes' recourse when faced with the need to unencumber explanation in physics from the burden of mentalist conceptions and biological metaphors which it had borne from Greek beginnings forward. His most confident insight is the view that motions of bodies are a consequence of law-governed collisions among the particles of which the material order is composed. Thus we must expunge the substantial forms and occult qualities and other psychological inner determinants of change which figured in explanations of the scholastic-Aristotelian tradition. For Descartes explanations that advert to these concepts introduce soul-like agency into accounts of the motions of inanimate material things.

The basic motif of Descartes' thought, therefore, is not a conception of "mind" that places it outside spatial physical reality, but rather a conception of "body" that dictates the deletion of intentions, purposes, and thought from our ideas about physical individuals and events. He traces our inveterate indulgence in a defective mixture of mental and physical thinking to confusions retained from childhood. He offers a remarkable hypothesis to account for our susceptibility to this fallacious psychologism. Our propensity to this error is a manifestation of a self-protective disposition that is needed in childhood for the survival and well-being of the individual before his understanding and reason have developed.[2] Descartes therefore proposed a once-in-a-lifetime reassessment of each person's own thinking not simply as an exhortation to the method of doubt and the discipline of the clear and distinct foundations. It is also his prescription for an intellectual coming of age in which we can put childish patterns of thinking behind us.

The *res cogitans* that figures so prominently in the *Meditations* is the foundation of his reconstruction of human knowledge from the viewpoint of the subjectivity Descartes develops. His ideas about the physical world, however, determine the overall shape of this thinking. Descartes is the discoverer of egocentric subjectivity and the inventor of the epistemological program that starts from the contents of the mind and must argue for the very existence of material things. But the idea of mental substance is not an expression of Descartes' clearest, or most original, or best thinking. He does not advance philosophical psychology through the introduction of a distinct metaphysical foundation for conscious mentality. It is physical events that are brought into a clearer light when the mind has been swept aside into its own questionable substance. Far from clearing up anything, the mind, in itself, creates mysteries and perennial problems, the problem of the interconnection of the mental and the material being the most prominent of them.

The "piece-of-wax" discussion in the second Meditation expresses Descartes' own recognition of the relative insecurity of his thinking about the mind. Having "proved" that the thinker's own existence as a conscious being and the existence of the contents of his conscious mind are the first items that can be secured against the devastating method of doubt (and the only truths that he can *ever* secure without complex theological premises), Descartes introduces the wax discussion in anticipation of the understandably wary reader who will not easily give up the view that the familiar perceivable material things around him are surely better understood than is this strange speculation that makes "the mind more easily known than the body." In this passage Descartes is appreciative of the merit of a commonsense skepticism as opposed to his hyperbolic methodological skepticism that leads to hyperbolic and dubious "certainties." Surely our thinking is more stable and more reliable when we concern ourselves with the humble objects that we handle everyday, the things that litter our tables, like the wax that we melt in preparation for sealing our letters. How can our cognitive grasp of a *res cogitans* be accorded a more secure place in our understanding of reality than our knowledge of this ordinary cube of sealing wax? An awkward and all-too-philosophical flavor is unmistakable in the idea of mental stuff and our supposed foundational knowledge of it.

Of course, Descartes takes on this commonsense reaction only to face it down and to insist on his order of thinking, the order of thinking which became the standard agenda for modern philosophy. I mean to suggest that from the outset the idea of a nonmaterial substance as the metaphysical housing for conscious mental life has been promoted by pressures from nonmental subject matters that we do understand, as Descartes understood mechanical explanation in physics. Little light has ever been cast on psychological things by accepting the dualist idea.

Modern materialists have been so profoundly convinced by the general structure of Cartesian thinking about the mind that they manage to promote only a materialist version of a philosophy of mind that is essentially Cartesian in its underlying attitudes and in extensive matters of detail. Contemporary mind-brain materialism is a body-body dualism. Materialists typically accept the Cartesian idea of an inner mental realm. Contemporary repudiation of dualism is generally a consequence of the extension of scientific knowledge in the biological field and the acceptance of a comprehensive evolutionary naturalism. Many thinkers now sympathize with the materialist rejection of mental substance. Impenetrable mysteries will be a part of understanding the mind as long as a ghostly substratum for consciousness and mental activity is tolerated.

But the materialist sees little further than this broad metaphysical issue. Identity theory insists on the material character of mental items. Forgetting Descartes' good reasons for expelling the mental from the world of physical events, materialists cancel the real intellectual gains that he secured in segregating psychological explanations from our thinking about material objects and the causes of motions. Materialism offers no compensating advantages at all for the rehabilitation of the psychologism that Descartes managed to eliminate from physics.

Of course, the development of sciences that seem to be related to mental functioning, such as neurophysiology, information theory, and artificial intelligence, encourage the materialist philosopher of mind that his "hypothesis" is the way of science. The recent readmission of mind and consciousness to a material standing is motivated by the same global demands of science as its original expulsion from the material world. Where Descartes argued that thoughts, intentions, beliefs, and desires *must be* nonphysical entities lest we impute mind-like functions to mere material things and inanimate interactions, the preponderance of contemporary philosophers of mind, and Donald Davidson most clearly and influentially, hold that these mental items *must be* physical realities in the brain because they are among the causes of physical events (actions), and only physical causes can have physical effects. In Davidson's case, at least, the "anomalousness" of his monism is equivalent to a frank admission that the gain in understanding that will accrue from accepting his monistic philosophy of mind is nil.

Materialism is on the wrong track because the trouble with Cartesian philosophy of mind lies in its conception of a realm of inner mental things and events comprising conscious mentality. This is the aspect of Cartesianism that is retained by materialists to this very day. So the chief defect of materialism, in my view, is that it is a species of Cartesian philosophy of mind.

2. Identifying conscious phenomena

Materialist and dualist "theories" answer to a felt need for some kind of account of consciousness. There are states of consciousness, and all men are familiar with them. But there is a lot of confusion and uncertainty as to what these states of consciousness are from a theoretical, or from a metaphysical, or from a scientific point of view. The mind-brain identity theory offers us an understanding, or at least a proposal, concerning what these states of consciousness with which we are all familiar actually are.[3] Here is an analogy: Bright twinkling points of light in the night sky constitute a range of phenomena with which men are familiar. The bright-point-star identity theory proposes to tell us what these bright points actually are, namely, distant, massive physical bodies rather like the sun.

So far I mean to say that in our conception of the need for a theory about consciousness we tend to construe consciousness in terms of a range of phenomena, and then a theory of consciousness, like any other theory, is an effort to account for the phenomena of that range. I will argue that the trouble with the mind-brain theory is not the materialist identification of states of consciousness that it makes but the fact that, like other theories of consciousness, it is based on the preliminary idea that consciousness can be thought of in terms of phenomena to be accounted for. The identity theory relies upon this preliminary idea. Once it is accepted that consciousness is a matter of phenomena to be accounted for, the phenomena have to be identified in one way or another, and in our climate of thought any nonmaterialist identification is *prima facie* exotic and suspect.

Is the materialist theory as an identification of conscious phenomena idiosyncratic? Is the idea that we face a range of conscious phenomena something that arises with the materialist inspiration in the philosophy of mind? Or is the demand for identification something that is characteristic of traditional philosophical thinking about consciousness and, perhaps, everyday thinking as well? We have to say that the materialist theory is not at all radical or innovative in this respect. Rather, identity theory fits snugly into a traditional philosophical pattern and differs in its account of consciousness only in the metaphysical status to which it assigns conscious states and not at all in the preliminary conception of these states as phenomena which must be assigned some metaphysical status. Identity theorists themselves recognize that they do not differ from dualist or idealist philosophers of mind in thinking of consciousness in terms of a range of data calling for a theoretical account, and that they do differ only in the theoretical account that they give. So, for example, J.J.C. Smart employs the phrase "immediate experience" to designate what he calls "inner goings-on" which a man can report on and compare with one another, and he says, "the dualist would construe these goings-on as goings-on in an immaterial substance, whereas the materialist would construe these goings-on as taking place inside our skulls."[4] In the same spirit, the items that U.T. Place identifies with brain events are, in his words, the subject matter of "reports" and "introspective observations,"[5] while David Armstrong calls them objects of "inner sense."[6] Smart, Place, and Armstrong, then, correctly reflect the historical continuity of mentalist and materialist thinking about consciousness. A materialist identity theory offers an account of the same range of phenomena as dualism; it merely offers a different account.

3. Consciousness and inner states and processes

The identity theorists' use of "inner sense," "introspection," and "inner goings-on" also brings out an affinity with traditional philosophical thought about consciousness as *inner*. We might compare John Locke, for example, who says that consciousness is "perceiving what is going on in one's own mind."[7] The difference between traditional dualist accounts of consciousness and modern materialism comes down to the question "How far *inside* is the mind?" Materialists stop at the brain, while dualists press on further inward to find a locus of the phenomena of consciousness. In fact, the thought that consciousness consists in the occurrence or presence of things inside is precisely the thought of consciousness as a range of phenomena, namely, these inner presences or occurrences for which we need some kind of account. For reference, let us call this conception of the need for a theory about consciousness *the idea of the phenomena of consciousness*.

No philosopher asserts that the phenomena of consciousness are objects of sense perception. No one says that we literally see our states of consciousness or hear our mental activities going on. The phenomena are not *given* to us in the way in which the twinkling points of light in the night sky are given to us, for we do see the twinkling points of light that are later identified with massive hot bodies like the sun. However, the vocabulary of common sense and of philosophical tradition is dependent upon the language of perception for a means of expressing figuratively how it is that conscious states are phenomena at all, that is, how it is that we know about them and are familiar with them, and, thus, how we need some theory about the nature of them to begin with. As quoted, Locke said that we do perceive what goes on in our minds, although he did not, of course, mean perceive by way of the senses. Hume, to take another example, in his famous discussion of personal identity also speaks of "entering into himself most intimately" in the effort to "observe" himself, which he notoriously fails to do.[8] His failure, however, contrasts with his success in observing his own perceptions, which means, in his terminology, his conscious states. Descartes also speaks of "inspection" by the mind of its contents, namely, "ideas," which are conscious elements of the mental life for him. Kant speaks of "empirical self-consciousness" to cover receptivity to inner objects. Thus, although these philosophers differ among themselves in important respects, and though they differ even more from contemporary materialist philosophers of mind, they all share a general notion of the phenomena of consciousness. They fall easily into the metaphorical language of perception and observation and things we can report on in order to express the manner in which we are apprised of this range of phenomena.

All this attests to the naturalness of the idea of the phenomena of consciousness. For phenomena should be some kind of given things. Phenomena contrast essentially with things that figure in hypotheses, or things the existence of which is posited, assumed, or a matter of plausible conjecture. Phenomena are what we know about in some fundamental and indisputable way, and so for that reason we feel the need for a theory that will make conceptual room for and account for such things. Phenomena are what theories must *save*. The language of perception provides a metaphorical vehicle for expressing our access to the phenomena of consciousness that will be saved by a theory of consciousness.

The very idea of the phenomena of consciousness converts states of consciousness and conscious activities into *objects of consciousness*. Phenomena, inner states, ongoing inner processes, and all objects of inspections, observations, introspections, and inner quasi-perceptions have to be things of which we can be conscious. I think that this is usually conceded by theorists of consciousness, to the extent that this thought is addressed at all. Thus, Smart says that a man's reports on his conscious states are reports on inner goings-on, and that a man can tell others when it is that these things go on in him, and that he can find these ongoing inner matters like and unlike one another.[9] Smart can only say these things on the assumption that these inner goings-on are objects of consciousness. Only on this understanding could Smart find himself in agreement with dualists on everything except the metaphysical status and location of inner goings-on and thus promote a topic-neutral terminology for describing these realities.

What is wrong with simply allowing this? Why not just say that conscious states are objects of consciousness, that they are among the things of which we are conscious? Some objects of consciousness such as outer material objects do not puzzle us, and they seem to be susceptible to scientific treatment. But these inner objects with which we are familiar and on which we can report are puzzling and threaten to fall outside the patterns of scientific understanding we have at hand. *Being conscious* of something is what puzzles us. The right identification of the thing of which we are conscious does not solve the puzzle. It is not the objects of consciousness but the fact of consciousness that is mysterious and hard to connect with a scientific outlook. Men are not simply related to other things in the world and participants in complex events with things in the world. Men are also conscious of things in the world and of themselves and, to some extent, of their situation in the world. Now it will not do to try to shed light on this by saying only that man is aware of two kinds of things and not just one kind of thing, that he is aware of inner goings-on as well as being aware of outer realities. For to say that there is more that men are conscious of than the outer world, to say that beyond this outer scope there is another inner scope of consciousness, does not help us with the question "How is it that men are conscious at all, conscious of things within any scope?"

Just because it tries to be scientific and unsentimental, the mind-brain theory could help us to bring out this difficulty with special force. Assume that the identity theory is correct. All these inner events with which men have always been familiar are identical with events in the brain. These things that Locke said that he perceived, that Descartes inspected, and that Hume found within when he was looking for *himself*, we will now suppose are material things, physical states and processes, and none of them are queer ethereal or spiritual states or entities, as so many philosophers have been tempted to think in the past. If we accept this, what is gained? Just because these objects are no longer mysterious things, assuming the success of materialism, it ought to be easy to see that their identification is irrelevant to an account of our consciousness of them.

Let us reconsider for the sake of comparison, the bright-point-star identity theory. Suppose that in the past some people under the influence of prescientific ideas thought that the bright points in the night sky were angels and not material things at all. We could tell such folk,

> Those outer things of which you are aware and that you take
> to be nonmaterial angels are actually identical with massive,
> distant, hot bodies like the sun.

But this assertion, be it ever so firmly established, could not be supposed to advance our understanding of consciousness. A person who accepts this informative identification cannot be expected to react by saying,

> Now I understand my consciousness of those bright points
> of light. I did not know they were material things. I thought
> they were something spiritual.

In exactly the same way, if some of the objects of our consciousness
are inner objects, and we suspect, confusedly perhaps, that these inner objects are nonmaterial realities, our consciousness of them is not
made intelligible by the proposition that they are material goings-on
after all, and if he accepts this news, it is still not reasonable to expect
someone to respond to the theory saying,

> Now I understand consciousness. I thought it had some non-
> material objects and some material objects, but I see now
> that they are all material objects, some inner and some outer.

The nature of the objects of consciousness is one question. The nature
of consciousness is another. The very idea of conscious *phenomena*
systematically conflates the two questions.

4. Luminosity

An identification of the character of an object of consciousness,
even a correct identification, does not clarify the concept of consciousness itself. No doubt it is for this reason that both dualism and materialism seem to disappoint the expectations for explanation that theories
ordinarily carry with them. This is a simple point, and yet it reveals
undetected deficiencies in the general thinking of identity theorists,
whether they propose a material or nonmaterial identification of conscious mental states. To understand how such fundamental irrelevance
goes unnoticed, let us turn once again to traditional philosophical
thought about consciousness.

Materialist identity theories and dualist theories have prospered
to the extent that they have succeeded in blurring that distinction that
I want to stress. Many philosophers of mind promote, either explicitly
or tacitly, the view that a distinction between the objects of our consciousness and our consciousness of them does not apply when we are
talking about those inner goings-on that make up the phenomena of
consciousness. The elimination of the distinction between objects and
consciousness is explicit, for example, in the Berkeleyan formula *"Esse
is percipi."* Consciousness of the object somehow constitutes the very
being of the object of consciousness. If this can be so, then to account

for what we are conscious of is to account for consciousness itself. If we could accept any such view, then theories like the mind-brain materialist's could be rescued. So let us call this the *rescuing clause*.

Materialism would be rescued if we could say of these inner objects of consciousness which we inspect, observe, and report on that for these special objects there is just no difference between this happening in us and our being aware of this happening. These inner goings-on, unlike others, and unlike all outer goings-on, are themselves conscious goings-on. So perception is indeed a misleading metaphor for our means of being acquainted with the phenomena of consciousness. Actually we have no such means, and we require none. The phenomena of consciousness, being conscious phenomena, do not need to be surveyed at all in order that they be objects of consciousness. Descartes, Locke, and Hume speak of inspecting, perceiving, and observing the inner; Place, Smart, and Armstrong speak of introspecting, reporting on, and sensing the inner. But all this is metaphor. According to the rescuing clause there is no such thing as, nor need for, inspecting or introspecting, observing or sensing for inner phenomena that are already conscious in virtue of their very constitution.

It is exactly this rescuing clause that is needed for any theory of consciousness that uses the idea of the phenomena of consciousness. Without this clause the identification of the inner objects of consciousness is as irrelevant to the understanding of consciousness as the identification of outer objects of consciousness. Identity theorists, dualist or materialist, are all subject to this fundamental criticism unless they suppose that when it comes to conscious phenomena, there is no question of detecting, observing, or even introspecting the phenomena because the phenomena are intrinsically conscious. Using an apter metaphor than perception, the rescuing clause says that conscious phenomena are "luminous" and that, as such, they do not need to be illuminated. Let us call this the idea of the luminous phenomena of consciousness.

There is a general appreciation of the need for this move to luminous phenomena in the generation of philosophical theories about consciousness. Some philosophers recognize that we do not want to generate more inner objects of consciousness but that the phenomena we account for ought to be, in some sense, our awarenesses themselves. Thus, in connection with perception, which is after all an instance of as well as a metaphor for conscious activity, many but by no means all philosophers realize that we cannot construe perceptual consciousness in terms of a second, parallel but inner, object of consciousness. It is our *seeings,* our *hearings,* and, more theoretically, our *being appeared to* in this or that way that carries the idea of perceptual consciousness. But these conceptions of the subject matter for philosophical scrutiny in perception are commonly converted back into inner objects of consciousness by the constraints of the theories which philosophers entertain as options in accounting for perceptual consciousness.

Materialists think that it is not a lemonlike object that will be identified with a neural entity but a seeing of a lemon, or, in Smart's terminology, "its looking to the subject as though there is a lemon there in front of him." Something queer happens in the passage of thought that tries to focus on these conceptions of our perceivings and awarenesses. In spite of the good intentions of the theorist in trying not to engender another inner object of consciousness, his seeings and havings of impressions turn into inner objects of consciousness very quickly. This is because the seeings and havings, although billed as our awareness of things, are still regarded as matters on which a subject reports. The sensuous character of outer objects of perception is deleted by the move to "seeings" and "havings," but this merely yields an inner object reported on that does not seem to have any describable features. Still the subject is supposed to know when one of these things is going on in him. He is supposed to know, at least, that they are like and unlike one another, that all seeings of lemons have something in common, that seeings have features unlike hearings, and so on. But all this requires the idea of inner realities on which subjects report because they are aware of these realities. So the effort to address consciousness itself rather than inner objects seems to fail.

5. Luminosity in foundational epistemology

Those epistemologists and philosophical psychologists who found the idea of sense data and sense impressions essential to their thinking did posit inner sensuous objects of consciousness in perception. Almost all thinkers who employed these ideas took them to be inner objects that contrast with the things in our spatial environment that we speak of perceiving from a preanalytic point of view. In keeping with what we have said so far, the introduction of sense data, or of

any related concept of sensuous inner objects in perception, does not
in itself shed light on the consciousness of perception of any objects
apprehended, whether inner or outer. Something like the rescuing
clause would be needed to move from any theory of inner objects of
consciousness to an account that addresses the nature of consciousness.
In other words, the inner objects of perceptual consciousness must be
thought of as luminous phenomena. Historically the luminosity of objects of perceptual consciousness has been achieved through confused
appeal to the incorrigibility of reports on inner, as opposed to outer,
objects of perceptual consciousness, and/or through appeal to the infallibility of the subject with respect to his own inner objects of perceptual consciousness.

The claim of incorrigibility or infallibility, which is fortunately
no longer much pressed by analysts of perception, corresponded to
the epistemological objective, the need to find an unshakeable foundation for empirical knowledge claims, which empiricists inherited from
Descartes. Perhaps the seeming need for incorrigibility would not have
so easily engendered the claim that we enjoy incorrigibility were it not
for the fact that certain familiar epistemological moves seemed to yield
claims about perceptual consciousness which are, in fact, insulated from
most of the liabilities of ordinary perception claims. Philosophers' formulations produced "reports" sufficiently insulated to appear to be
incorrigible. At one time many philosophers valued subjective reports
hedged around with clauses like "I may be hallucinating or I may be
seeing an external object but in any case, I make out something such
that. . . ." The idea was that such guardedness might preserve an irreducible grain of pure phenomenal knowledge from which the total
edifice of human knowledge, and science in particular, might be constructed or reconstructed.

As in this report of what "I may be seeing or hallucinating, but
in any case . . . ," sense data or other inner objects of such claims were
sometimes *defined* as sensuous objects such that if the subject thinks
they are present, they are present, and if the subject thinks they are
not present, then they are not. According to this definition it seems
that the inner objects of perceptual consciousness must be luminous.
If it is the case that, by definition, a subject is conscious of them when
they exist in him, then there is no question of a process of observation
or detection which could fail. On these principles it will be impossible to be inattentive enough to miss one's own sense data.

There is, of course, no arguing with definitions. If sense data are defined as luminous inner objects of perceptual consciousness, why that is just what they are. It is strange, however, that philosophers should ever have thought that much could be gained through the introduction of definitions such as this. The idea was supposed to be that because sense data are *this sort of object*, our reports of them are absolutely secure. Though sense data have gone out of fashion, I think it was never brought out clearly that this kind of definition cannot serve any purpose whatever in epistemological projects. The use that was projected for these definitions betrays a confusion about luminosity.

We can see the epistemological bankruptcy of such definitions of sense data by comparing them with definitions of outer objects of perceptual consciousness. Let us suppose that we are interested in the absolute security of our reports. A subject reports, "I see a lemon." This is hardly a foundation claim or a formulation of ultimate evidence within the framework of the old epistemological tradition. Why not? Well, the thing may not be a lemon. It may be cardboard or plaster. It may contain no lemon juice. It may not have grown on a lemon tree. Any philosopher would snort at the idea that these liabilities in a report of perception might be eliminated by a definition of the object such as

> A lemon is, *by definition*, a piece of fruit that has grown
> on a lemon tree, and is not made of plaster, or cardboard,
> and has lemon juice in it, and. . . .

Maybe these things are true of lemons by definition. In any event, philosophers might stipulate that their own use of "lemon" will be governed by such a definition. This is not a matter of argument. But theory of knowledge is not advanced here because the definition is impotent to assure us that a thing made out on some occasion is one of these wonderful objects that *must* come from a tree and *must* contain lemon juice. Definition cannot guarantee that the thing I make out in front of me fits the definition. No definition can show that something I apprehend is not a pasteboard construction, much less a merely optical phenomenon. If my report "I see a lemon" is challenged, no one will accept the defense "Of course, it grew on a tree. Lemons grow on trees by definition." In just the same way, "Of course, it is yellow and oval in shape. It is a sense datum, and sense data have all the features they appear to have, by definition" cannot defend a report someone makes. We are free to define things as we please. But no definition can provide assurance for the claim that something of which we are conscious fits one definition rather than another. How do we know that this object is yellow, given that it looks yellow? Well, it is a sense datum, and they are as they look by definition. But then how do we know it is a sense datum? Surely we cannot get that, too, from the definition. And if not from the definition, then from what quarter will our confidence that this thing is a sense datum come?

To sum up this point, some philosophers have tried to attach the claim of luminousness to an inner sensuous object of perceptual consciousness via the seeming incorrigibility of claims about inner objects such as sense data, while others have rejected the proliferation of inner objects and tried to concentrate on seeings and havings of sense experiences, and for these the seeings and havings become luminous inner realities. Neither of these procedures takes a step toward making the concept of luminosity intelligible, let alone credible. In both cases some version of the idea of the luminousness of the inner has to be invoked lest the theoretical content of the view collapse immediately into the idea that there are inner objects of consciousness, and, as we have said, that view does not even address the issue of consciousness itself.

On the one hand, for the sense-data picture of the inner object of perceptual consciousness the sensuous inner object has to be self-revealing. On the other hand, for the havings-of-sense-impressions picture of the inner object immediate experiences are nonsensuous inner processes, impossible to describe directly, and a subject matter for which we lack a phenomenological language. But in both cases the inner object which is a candidate for identification is something whose presence is reported on by the subject in whom it goes on or is present. In all of the welter of confusing and contradictory conceptions of the inner item in perception—sense data, sensa, percepts, appearances, appearings, ways of being appeared to, sense impressions, havings of sense impressions, and ongoing indescribable immediate experiences—the common thread is that this reality, however conceived, is something of which a perceiver is aware or something on which he reports. If these concepts are to figure in an understanding of consciousness, the thesis of luminosity must be attached to them. This is inevitable, for any conception of objects of perceptual consciousness which does not include this rescuing device will not be an account of consciousness at all.

6. The idea of the inner

I would like to introduce two speculative points here concerning the idea of luminous phenomena in consciousness by way of evaluation of the rescuing clause that employs this idea. In the move that winds up at the rescuing clause, here is what seems to happen. We start by finding consciousness of outer things remarkable. Naively our consciousness seems like a window. All the world is outside. Our clumsy, unofficial, and yet insistent thought about consciousness *puts* everything *out there*. It is all spatial, all mechanical, all cause and effect. If there are any other subjects of experiences, they are not constituents of the outer world, but they are, rather, further windows opening onto it. The hard-to-articulate sense of one's own presence as the subject apprehending what is out there, the sense of being *oneself* and not just another constituent in the system of things, this sort of *awakeness to things* even to oneself—this is not out there with objects of consciousness that exhaust reality. Consciousness itself is, in some awkward way, *in here*, looking out of the window on the far side of which lies the whole of reality, everything that is. Consciousness cannot be something out in the world simply because consciousness takes in all of that world and implies something like a distance from or a perspective on what is accessible to consciousness.

This is murky, yet it has something to do with the intuitive foundation of the innerness of the mental. The spatial order of objects of perception is paradigmatically outer. This is a fundamental Cartesian conviction. The spatial, where everything is locatable with respect to everything else, is the motif for objects of consciousness. Consciousness itself cannot be located in this space. Perhaps this seems wrong because the perspective of visual perception involves a point from within the space of perceived objects, a point of origin for perceptual experiences at which the perceiver is located. But for consciousness proper, perceptual experiences, each with its own built-in viewpoint, are themselves objects of experience. Both the space of the perceived and the viewpoint of the perceiver are incorporated in the object of perceptual consciousness, the perceptual experience. So consciousness withdraws itself from the point occupied by the sense organs of the perceiver as much as from the region occupied by the object perceived. The process of perception is what seems to be conscious. Mere perceived objects like lemons have nothing to do with consciousness. From this viewpoint experiences, not lemons, are objects of consciousness in perception, and experiences are not spatial objects. This is the inner world.

The dualist then continues, "If inner, then not spatial, and if not spatial, then surely not material!" There is a certain validity to this thought, shaky as it is, and hedged with such uncertain metaphors. Once it is introduced into our thinking, the inner becomes more than the point of origin of the perspective of our consciousness of things, a point which has to lie outside the locus of things on which we have a perspective. The inner becomes a *region* in which further objects of consciousness can be thought to reside. In the skeptical solipsistic tradition another step is taken that limits consciousness to inner objects and makes all outer objects subject matter for hypothesis and not objects of awareness at all. This potent tradition has the ironic feature that philosophers, having started from the desire to explain man's godlike capacity to know the world, reach the solipsistic conclusion that denies that he has any such capacity, since his world is all hypothesis and not object of consciousness!

Whether we accept the solipsist's viewpoint or not, the rescuing clause requires us to take seriously the concept of inner phenomena of consciousness, and also requires that we think of such inner objects as intrinsically conscious phenomena. All the difficulties that we feel in the notion of consciousness are thus concentrated by the rescuing clause in this impenetrable feature, namely, that they are automatically and intrinsically conscious. This impenetrability is not in the least mitigated by the supposedly scientific information that such luminous phenomena are brain events. So in order to continue in the stance of theorists trying to account for phenomena, both mentalists and materialists have to incorporate everything problematic in the bare notion of the phenomena they are going to account for. Having done that, the mere assertion that the phenomena in question have this or that metaphysical status, even if we had reason to think such an assertion true, can accomplish very little. Therefore, the rescuing clause does not rescue much. Ultimately, this is the reason for the explanatory poverty of dualism and the inherited explanatory poverty of subsequent "corrections" of dualism by materialist philosophy of mind.

7. Luminosity and the physiological viewpoint

The second speculative point I would like to introduce is centered on the notion of innerness. Innerness creates an ambience of the elusive and indefinite without which the rescuing clause would not be at all attractive or appear to offer an insight into something. The rescuing clause is the assertion that the inner phenomena in question are luminous, so that there is no question of doing anything even metaphorically like perceiving them. We would be bewildered by the claim that any outer object had this feature, and I believe that we rely entirely on the fuzziness and the shifting focus of our notion of innerness in order to avoid the same bewilderment when the claim of luminousness is made for inner objects.

Berkeley said that philosophers raise a dust and then complain that they cannot see. But the idea of inner objects raises a dust which enables philosophers to believe that through the dust they can just dimly make out something where the impossibility of such a thing is quite apparent in the absence of the dust. When objects of consciousness are inner objects, philosophers can contemplate the suggestion that their existence and our consciousness of them are one and the same thing. We are willing to suppose that this is just how it is with these luminous events of which our consciousness is actually composed. I do not mean that there are no inner objects of consciousness. To the extent that we find it right to speak of inner objects of consciousness I think we do need an analogy for perception of them. Again, the mind-brain identity theory might help us to see this point, but in fact it has not done so because of the retention of essentially Cartesian ideas in the governing thinking of materialists.

If we adopt a physiological attitude toward the inner, and that ought to be the *sine qua non* of a materialist philosophy of mind, we should emphasize the need for a physiological explanation of our consciousness of things within. Of course, a lot goes on in our bodies of which we have no awareness at all. But a few things that go on inside us are objects of conscious experience. All the sensitive zones of the interiors of our bodies are, *per se*, regions within which we can be aware of inner events and processes. But there is always, in the offing, a physiological explanation of our consciousness of these things. This is the essence of the physiological viewpoint when it comes to perception and other forms of awareness of things inside or outside. Suppose, for example, we ask a physiologist how it is that we are aware of things inside us, how we are able to feel things such as unpleasant goings-on in our decaying teeth. Imagine that a physiologist should answer,

> Well, when something goes on in your teeth, it's just an intrinsically conscious event. That is how it is with tooth events. They are what I call "luminous." As phenomena, occurrences in your teeth are conscious phenomena.

I do not think that such an answer would strike us as consistent with, much less as demanded by, science. But it is the only answer open to the materialist identity theorist when it comes to brain events, as construed by the rescuing clause. How is it that we are able to be aware of these events in our brains? How is it that we find ourselves in a position to report their presence and find them like and unlike one another? How do we know that these things go on "in typical situations"? The brain, after all, is one of the insensitive parts of the human body. The brain is not anesthetized in brain surgery. For the philosophical identity theory all the physiological explanatory stories, that is, the stories of perceptual and proprioceptive sensitivity, and of transmission of information in the nervous system, are told in accounting for the mere occurrence of the brain event. The brain is, by hypothesis, the end of the line for these stories. That means that the only answer available to the mind-brain materialist when asked how we manage to be aware of these brain events is:

> Well, when something like that goes on in your brain, it is just intrinsically conscious. There is no *way* in which you are conscious of these things, as though you had another nervous system for apprehending what goes on in this one. Such brain events are simply conscious phenomena. You might call them "luminous." There is no physiological story to be told here. That is just how it is with such brain events.

This impenetrable bruteness of consciousness when it is thus incorporated in its own object in the case of brain events also makes it just as brute and incomprehensible that other inner events such as the flow of blood in the capillaries of the toes are not luminous. For there is nothing about the brain events qua physical events that makes it seem suitable that they should be intrinsically conscious realities while other events should unfold in darkness.

Physiology does not endorse or encourage the idea of luminous conscious mental phenomena in any way whatsoever. In fact, the idea that the brain is insensitive means that it does not fall within the scope of the receptors which make it possible for us to be aware of events in the extremities and outside in the world. So we are not conscious of anything going on in the brain, although a great deal that is essential to our consciousness and to our overall mental functioning does go on in it. The pattern of physiological explanation for sensitivity and perception does not prepare us in the least for the idea that some phenomena are just intrinsically conscious, so that there is no question of becoming conscious of them. One might hope, in view of this, that in adopting a standpoint that is supposed to profit from affiliation with neurophysiology the materialist identity theory would incline to give up the idea of luminous phenomena altogether. Materialist philosophers of mind, however, never do this, and instead, in the last analysis, they give up the physiological viewpoint, that is, the assumption that there is a physiological explanation of our awareness of whatever we are aware of. In this the materialist is no worse than the mentalist. The two theories are on exactly the same footing. As an intellectual product, the materialist theory is stranger than the mentalist, because the nonmaterial mind raises a much denser and more effective dust than materialism, so that the latter cannot do nearly as good a job at masking the spuriousness of the rescuing clause.

Even with the rescuing clause the idea of the phenomena of consciousness cannot generate sensible theories about consciousness, since the rescuing clause simply conceals all the difficulties about consciousness in the mere concept of intrinsically conscious phenomena. The rescuing clause essentially relies on the mysteriousness of the inner, whether material or mental, in order to confer a spurious appearance of intelligibility on the concept of intrinsically conscious phenomena. If the concept of luminosity invoked by the rescuing clause is abandoned, then it appears that philosophical accounts of consciousness cannot be accounts of phenomena of any sort at all.

8. The rôle of inner-conscious phenomena

Let us set aside suspicions about luminosity and examine the work done by the concept of inner-conscious phenomena in our thinking about experience. It is fitting to pay special attention to perceptual consciousness, because the metaphor of perception figures so prominently in the idea of inner objects of consciousness, and because thought based on the idea of perceptual consciousness has played such a decisive rôle in metaphysical and epistemological programs since the Renaissance.

We can start from Descartes' example of perceptual consciousness of a piece of wax. What is the object of consciousness in a subject's conscious visual perception of a shiny red cube of wax? One promising answer is that the piece of wax is the object of consciousness here, the piece of wax construed, not as a construct out of private data, but as a material thing existing outside the perceiver. However, insofar as this is the object of consciousness, the object is certainly not an intrinsically conscious phenomenon. We cannot say of a piece of wax that by its very existence we are conscious of it. More conspicuously, a piece of wax is not an ethereal event in the mind, nor, failing that, is a piece of wax something material that occurs in or goes on in the brain. So if we thought that *the only thing* that a man is conscious of when he sees a piece of wax is the piece of wax itself, then we would not have provided a field of operation, so far, for mentalist or for materialist philosophers of mind. This is not because theorists of consciousness do not mean to cover perceptual consciousness in their theories. On the contrary, the traditional and current literatures of identity theories abound in perceptual illustrations, and perception of outer objects is as prominent as ever in the writings of contemporary materialist philosophers of mind.

Most philosophers think that there is a conscious phenomenon involved when somebody sees something, at least in those cases when the subject is paying attention to what he sees and can describe the object and answer questions based on the presumption that he sees it. The conscious phenomenon in such a case is, of course, not what the perceiver sees. The inner thing which is offered as a conscious phenomenon, and which is to be identified with something material if not with an ethereal reality, is, let us say, a seeing of a piece of wax, or a visual experience of a piece of wax. A seeing of a cube of wax sounds like something that might go on in a person, and something of which a man might be thought conscious, since he can say whether or not it is going on. For that matter it also sounds like something that might turn out to be a brain event. Finally, seeing a piece of wax may even have the desired feature of luminosity. For when a seeing of a piece of wax takes place in a subject, it might be right to say that he is simply aware that it does. He does not have to survey his seeings as though by some inner analog of perception. So seeings are among the phenomena which theorists of perceptual consciousness propose to identify. Just here it does seem unsentimental and scientific to say, "Seeings are actually brain events." But all of this is a kind of grammatical ilusion, and we have not earned the right to identify seeings as conscious phenomena at all.

Suppose that the bit of wax is at least one thing of which the subject is conscious on some occasion when he sees a bit of wax. Imagine questioning this subject: "Is seeing a piece of wax taking place in you?" we ask him. How is he to answer? Won't he say, "Do you mean, Can I see the wax? If not, what do you mean?" We philosophers may have to encourage our informants. "You know, are you having the visual experience of seeing a piece of wax? The thing that is conscious in perception of a piece of wax?" Trusting a normal degree of cooperativeness, and assuming that our man does see the wax and has no philosophical theory of his own to push, I think he will be induced to agree that he has the experience. But does this tend to show us that he is aware of more than one thing? Is it not necessarily the case that if he sees the wax, and if that is an object of his consciousness, that by itself will determine the answer "Yes, I have the experience. Seeing of the wax is present in me, or occurring in me"? I mean that we put the question "Is a conscious experience going on?" as though to ask about something inner, but it will surely be answered only in terms of the outer. If not, we have to envision a situation in which the man sees the wax, and is conscious of the wax, and yet does not have the experience, that is, that seeing a piece of wax does not take place in him. I do not seriously think that we ever envision such a situation or that we have any way of making the idea of such a situation minimally intelligible to ourselves. But if that is so, our inquiry about an inner object is illusory. Actually, the expression "his seeing of the wax" is generated grammatically as the ever-available nominalization of "He sees the wax." This grammatical offspring does not indicate that there are always two objects of consciousness in visual perception, one an outer object and the other an inner experience. The assumption that our subject is conscious only of the shiny red cube, and of no inner process at all, does not inhibit the discussion of his perceptual consciousness.

We confuse ourselves here, in part, because we think of our experiences as filling stretches of time whose dimensions do not coincide with the temporal parameters of anything outer and objective. Our subject is seeing the cube of wax through a definite interval. The temporal specifications indicate *when* the subject was conscious of the wax and do not indicate another object of consciousness, an inner object in addition to the outer wax. If we were conscious of inner processes in perception, the question of the onset and duration of consciousness of those ongoing events would have to be answered. On that hypothesis we would have two sets of timings that we might compare as we compare the time of consciousness of the smell of roses and the time of inner allergic feelings that we believe the rose pollen causes in us. But, of course, we can make no sense at all of comparing the time of being conscious of the piece of wax I see and being conscious of the seeing of it. So seeings are only the grammatical product of consciousness of visible things and not further invisible objects of perceptual consciousness that raise special questions about their identification.

All this rests on the assumption that outer things are objects of consciousness. At this point we philosophers are notoriously susceptible to an adventurous line of thought based on the concept of an hallucination. Through adoption of this line, any perceptual experience will do as an illustration of something that could be an hallucination. The subject seeing the cube of wax could be just hallucinating. In such a case the subject's perceptual consciousness cannot be accounted for by appeal to an outer cube of wax because there is no outer object in an hallucination. But his perceptual consciousness will be exactly the same whether he perceives or hallucinates a piece of wax. This seems to fit very well with the identity theory and with the fact that hallucinations are to be made intelligible by appeal to neural occurrences.

Let us say that there are certain brain events that are normally brought about by a chain of causality starting from the external piece of wax but that are atypically brought about in the absence of a piece of wax in cases of hallucination. The neural occurrence goes on in the absence of the external piece of wax when we hallucinate, and so too, we think, the inner seeing, the conscious experience of a piece of wax, goes on without the wax when we hallucinate. The identity theory simply says that the inner events and the inner seeing are one and the same thing. This has seemed reasonable to many philosophers, and absolutely compelling to some. However, it is neither compelling nor reasonable.

To begin with we have to face the crucial question In the normal case are we to think that a man is conscious of an outer, shiny, opaque cube of wax and that he is also conscious of an inner object that is a seeing or a visual experience? Or are we to think that in the normal case, and in the hallucination, a man is conscious only of the inner process and that the difference lies only in the causal history of the true object of perceptual consciousness, which is an inner object in both cases? Rather than risk giving the wrong account on this crucial point, let us consider the two possible answers in turn. Our first account, then, will be that in normal perception a man is conscious of a piece of wax and also conscious of a seeing, while in hallucination only the seeing occurs in the perceiver. Our second account will be that in both normal and hallucinatory perceptual experience the only relevant object of consciousness is the inner object, the seeing which is caused in the normal case by the piece of wax and is caused in the hallucination in some other way. The reasonable-sounding line about hallucination rehearsed above is not actually a reasonable line because it depends on one or the other of these two accounts, and both of them are absurd.

The trouble with the first account is that it gives us two very different objects of consciousness in the normal case and only one of them in the hallucination. Yet, in invoking the idea of hallucination we are urged to think that a subject will somehow not notice, and not even be able to notice, that he has not the usual two very different objects of consciousness but only the inner one of them, which cannot itself be an object anything like the outer objects with which he is familiar when not hallucinating. This problem does not arise for the second account, for it gives us only one object of consciousness in perception, an object which is really there in us, whether we hallucinate or not. This second account relegates the piece of wax to a rôle in an hypothesis to explain the occurrence of the inner object of consciousness in the normal case. The trouble here is that in the framework of the second account such an hypothesis could not possibly be intelligible to us. Since we are never acquainted with anything but inner seeings and the like, and since these are nothing at all like pieces of wax—that is, they are not shiny, red, or cubical—we could have no way of attaching any significance to characterizations of outer things.

To see that this is so, we have to emphasize that the piece of
wax has these sensuous features while the inner ongoing experience
of seeing the piece of wax, since it is at least a candidate for identification with a neural reality in the brain, does not have these sensuous
features, for we cannot envision a shiny, red, cubical neural event.
Philosophers contemplating the materialist identity theory have often
seized on this extreme difference between seeings and outer things
seen, and they consistently recommend the difference as needed and
convenient for materialist thinking about conscious phenomena. The
gulf between features of seeings and features of outer objects is recognized, for example, by Smart, who says that the inner "immediate
experience" can only be described derivatively in terms of what goes
on in the subject when in "typical situations." Clearly, on Smart's understanding, recourse to derivative description is necessitated because
the inner ongoing experience does not itself have features like being
shiny and red, which would make it something describable through
directly using just this vocabulary. Cubes of wax certainly do not go
on in the subject and certainly do have all sorts of features that ongoing brain events will lack. The point, then, that we are accepting
from the materialist theory is that inner and outer objects of perceptual consciousness are very different kinds of objects, and only outer
objects have sensuous properties.

With this understanding, the absurdity of both projected lines
of thinking about hallucinations is overwhelmingly confirmed. On the
first account, in normal perception a subject is apprised of the presence
of two very different objects of consciousness, and one of them is a
sensuous object, while the other is an ongoing inner event that may
be identical with something in his brain. The former object is an outer
piece of wax, and the inner seeing is hard or impossible to describe
in terms of intrinsic features, but it definitely does not have sensuous
features. It would be a fallacy in the eyes of materialists to think otherwise. In hallucination, on this account, the usual inner object of consciousness is present, but there is no outer object, that is, no sensuous
object of consciousness at all. Nonetheless, we proposed in pursuing
this line on hallucination that the subject does not and cannot notice
that there is nothing shiny, red, and cubical that is an object of his
consciousness, but, instead, that he finds his situation indistinguishable
from the normal case. He does not say, "Hmmm, this is odd. Here's
this ongoing inner event that I usually get with pieces of wax, but there's
o piece of wax this time." On the contrary, in this account of hallucina-

tion a subject is overcome with a spirit of recklessness or unaccountable absentmindedness, and he judges that everything is as usual, while only one of the customary pair of very different objects of consciousness is present in him.

No doubt the fact that the inner ongoing event eludes any direct description carries a lot of the weight of this bizarre conception of hallucination. It manages this just because, as Smart notes, we will have to identify the inner "experience" in terms of a description of the outer object that normally occasions it, even though that description is not supposed to fit the inner object at all and cannot possibly fit the inner object if it is identical with a neural item. The need for a "derivative description" (Smart's phrase) means that the vocabulary for the outer will appear in designations of the inner such as "a seeing of a shiny, red cube of wax," and no other descriptive vocabulary will appear, thus generating the impression that the ongoing inner event might do in the explanation of an hallucination, even though it is not like a shiny, opaque, red, cubical thing in any way. If the inner object were directly describable at all, the proposed explanation of hallucination that invokes the anomalous occurrence of this inner item would immediately crumble. For it would be evident that no one could find the presence of a describable object of consciousness that is in no way like an outer perceived object indistinguishable from the perception which acquaints the perceiver with just such an outer object. The atypical occurrence of an inner event that usually accompanies conscious perception of a sensuous external object might give rise to the hypothesis that such an object is present but undetected, but that would not be an hallucination at all.

In other words, if we could put into words the features of these ongoing inner events of which philosophers suppose that we are conscious, then the absurdity of proposing that the presence of one of these inner occurrences in the absence of an outer object might be an hallucination would be apparent. Philosophers should be a good deal more skeptical about these inner objects that are alleged to be so familiar to us and yet totally indescribable in terms of features or character that they themselves actually possess.

Actually, the identity theory exploits the indescribability of the inner objects of consciousness in two ways. First, it is only because they are indescribable that we are able to entertain the thought that their occurrence might sometimes be hallucination. Were they describable at all, the unsuitableness of their descriptions for any outer object would make it evident that their occurrence could not conceivably be mistaken for sense perception. Second, being indescribable (apart from derivative "topic-neutral" descriptions that are not really descriptions at all) has the added convenience that these inner occurrences do not have features that might get in the way of any identification of them a philosopher might choose to make, and thus indescribable events will not embarrass a materialist identification.

This leaves us with the second option for interpreting inner conscious phenomena. That is the view that in both the normal and the aberrant case only the inner phenomenon is an object of consciousness and that the distinction between perception and hallucination concerns only the causal history of the things that are the inner objects of consciousness in both cases. This view avoids all the absurdities of the first interpretation, that is, of the account that admits two different objects of consciousness in normal and only one of them in indistinguishable aberrant perception, but it creates absurdities of its own that are equally devastating. On this interpretation it becomes reasonable to say that I mistake the aberrant for the normal case, that is, that I am deceived by an hallucination, even though in the aberrant case I am not conscious of anything that is shiny, opaque, red, and cubical. This is reasonable simply because on this second interpretation I am not aware of anything shiny, opaque, red, and cubical in the normal case either. The object of my consciousness in both cases is merely the ongoing inner event, and it does not have any such features since it is something that might turn out to be a brain event. On this understanding I am not ever conscious of something that has any sensuous characteristics. But then what sense could be attached to my hypothesis that a thing with sensuous characteristics has caused my inner conscious experience?

Time plays an especially prominent rôle in generating the conviction that there must be an inner object of perceptual consciousness. Surely something goes on in me when I see a piece of wax. I start seeing the wax at five before noon, I am still seeing it just before noon, and then at noon I see it no longer. Something started at five before noon, continued till noon, and then stopped. The wax cube did not start and stop. I am able to pronounce with unquestioned confidence and authority on the commencement and cessation of such things, so they seem to be matter for immediate awareness and non-inferential reports. It looks as though there is something going on in me, and I am conscious of it when it does go on. Shall we say that the thing timed here, the thing that lasts from 11:55 a.m. until noon, is my inner conscious seeing of the cube of wax?

Suppose that outer things were the only things of which a subject is ever aware. Suppose that he never notes anything starting or stopping inside him. Then this man offers no field of operation for an identity theorist vis-à-vis inner conscious experiences. Concerning objects of awareness such a subject is a complete extrovert. The things that he is aware of are all public outer things, and others are sometimes aware of the very same things. All this being allowed, we will still be able to ask this man *when* he is aware of the outer things of which he is aware. We will say, "When were you first aware of the cube of wax?" Such a subject would not deflect this question should he say, "I don't know anything about what goes on inside. I did not notice it start, so I couldn't tell you when it did start." He did notice the cube of wax, so he could tell us when he did notice *that*, and our question does not give him an excuse to change the subject as though we had inquired about an inner object and presumed him to be aware of it. As it is, people are aware of inner things and events, so they can time them. For instance, "My tooth started to ache after breakfast, and it has not stopped since." Being aware of something, one can say when one is aware of that thing, whether it is an outer or an inner thing. But then the timing of an awareness of an outer thing does not require the occurrence of an inner thing. We can say, "My seeing of the cube of wax lasted for five minutes," but this does not mean that I must have been conscious of something else besides the cube of wax, something that started and stopped inside me.

I will surely believe that something went on in my nervous system while I was aware of the wax. I have a rough appreciation of the physiology of perception, and I know that it would be magical were I to see things while my nervous system failed to function as it normally does in perception. Thus, neural events have the status here of theoretical occurrences, posited to explain the facts of perception and perceptual aberration. This status contrasts with that invoked by all identity theorists for whom inner events are not posits but objects of conscious experience that are merely identified by theory, for example, identified *as* neural events. When I hallucinate I can say, "Something very odd must be going on in my nervous system." I might say this not because I am consciously aware of events inside myself and I suppose, in a materialist spirit, that they must be physical events in my nervous system. Rather, I "perceive" something that does not exist, I need an explanation for this. It is the existence and not merely the neural character of inner events that is derived from theoretical considerations.

Philosophers of mind are perennially attracted to awkward phrases of which "his seeing of a cube of wax" is an illustration. These nominalizations are used as means of reference to inner experiences that are not encumbered by sensuous vocabulary. The wax is red, cubical, and shiny, but the seeing of it is none of these. Nominalization thus eliminates features which would conflict with a neural identification. In this passage of thought mere nominalization manages to change the subject under consideration from the outer to the inner, from the sensible to the nonsensible. The fact is that when we have buried all the descriptive terminology that actually fits anything we are aware of in a nominalization, the inner item "referred to" will certainly have no bothersome features that could embarrass any identification. Thus, the reason for which we are reduced to derivative description in trying to characterize Smart's immediate experiences is not that they are private and language has to be public but rather that the method of introducing the concept of the ongoing inner event has allocated all descriptive terminology to the outer reality of which we are actually aware and has generated an ongoing event under a heading like "it's looking to me that there is a yellow lemon." Nominalization is a grammatical engine that makes a new subject term out of a whole sentence. It is not an ontological engine that makes one object of perceptual consciousness into a whole new *subject matter*, a further object, that needs its own metaphysical allocation to mental or material realms. Since men see things at one time or another, temporal characterizations carry over to seeings of things. But this does not mean that seeings are further events of which subjects are conscious.

NOTES

1. For a discussion of the order of thinking that determines Descartes' views and the contrast with the order of thinking presented in the *Meditations* see A. Collins, "The Scientific Background of Descartes' Dualism," in *Thought and Nature*, Notre Dame, Indiana, 1985.

2. For example, in his reply to the sixth set of Objections assembled by Mersenne Descartes says, ". . . I noticed that from infancy I had passed various judgements about physical things, for example, judgements which

contributed much to the preservation of the life I was then entering; and I had afterwards retained the same opinions which I had before conceived touching these things. . . . And although the mind was at the time conscious of its own nature and possessed of an idea of thought as well as extension, nevertheless, having no intellectual knowledge, though at the same time it had an imagination of something, it took them to be one and the same and referred all its notions of intellectual matters to the body." E.S. Haldane and G.R.T. Ross, editors, *The Philosophical Works of Descartes*, London, 1911, vol. II, p. 254.

3. The same holds for the *functionalist* identity theory as a philosophy of mind. Although functionalism is the dominant philosophy of mind now, I will not address functionalism directly. I think of it as a form of materialism, even though functionalism does not address itself to the metaphysical hardware of mental or material substance, and even though some proponents of functionalism expressly say it is compatible with a dualist conception of the functional states with which mental phenomena are to be identified. In my view, which I will not defend here, the ideas of functionalism are burdened with obscurities and difficulties. Even if it is the case that functionalism itself is a neutral metaphysical thesis about mentality, the question of the metaphysical status of realizations of functional states will ultimately have to be faced, and we will get, perhaps, dualist functionalism and materialist functionalism. Since dualist functionalism will have the questionable merit of reintroducing the intractable problems of mind-body interaction that materialism tries to eliminate, I do not think that it will find many serious advocates among the scientifically minded to whom this kind of philosophy of mind has an appeal. Therefore, functionalism can be safely regarded as an effort in the philosophy of mind that will be, at the very least, coordinated with a materialist stand on realizations of functional states. As such it is a species of materialist thinking. In order to avoid comment on the subtle and very unsettled issues of functionalism here, I will address myself only to the materialist identification which will be a part of any functionalist theory that hopes to avoid the swamp of mental substance.

4. See J.J.C. Smart, "Materialism," *J. Phil.*, LX, 1963; as reprinted in C.V. Borst, *The Mind-Brain Identity Theory*, London, 1972, p. 162.

5. See U.T. Place, "Is Consciousness a Brain Process?" *Br. J. of Psych.*, LXVIII, 1956; as reprinted in Borst, pp. 47-51.

6. See, for example, David Armstrong, *A Materialist Theory of Mind*, London 1968, pp. 94-96 and esp. 323ff.

7. John Locke, *Essay Concerning Human Understanding*, II, i, 19.

8. See David Hume, *Treatise of Human Nature*, I, iv, 6.

9. J.J.C. Smart, "Materialism," and "Sensations and Brain Processess," *Phil. R.*, LXVIII, 1959, pp. 141-56.

V

Visual Experiences and Theoretical Identification

In contemporary discussions the principal assertions of a philosophy of mind are identifications of mental things such as sensations, beliefs, dreams, and perceptual experiences. In chapters 2 and 3 I have given reasons for rejecting the view that beliefs must be identified with some state of or event in a subject. For the present investigation I want to limit consideration of mental things to visual experiences, and I will take as representative of the currently debated philosophies of mind the assertion "Visual experiences are brain events." I call this kind of assertion a *theoretical identification*. In limiting consideration in this chapter to visual experiences I do not imply that all of the arguments presented and conclusions suggested here go over automatically into arguments and conclusions about other types of mental phenomena. In fact, I am sure that this is not the case. Visual experiences bring into focus ideas that are not relevant to other mental states, and other phenomena require attention to issues that do not arise in the context of perception. I do think that a conception of mental phenomena that is broadly conformable to the one I will present here concerning visual experiences can be developed for the philosophy of mind generally, but I will not defend this general contention here.

The discussion in this chapter has five parts: (1) the presumption of familiarity with the subject matter for which a theoretical identification appears to be needed; (2) the opposition between dualist and materialist conceptions of visual experiences at the pretheoretical level; (3) Thomas Nagel's view that the subjective eludes materialism and the generalization of this claim; (4) Saul Kripke's arguments against materialist philosophy of mind, responses to Kripke, and the generalization of Kripke's argument; (5) the thesis that there are no visual experiences and the explication of this idea.

1. What do theoretical identifications try to identify?

If I do not know what warts are, someone might tell me, "Warts are virus colonies." Like all identities, this one has two sides. The right side, here "virus colonies," is the theoretical side. In what follows I am more interested in the nontheoretical left side of the identity, in this case "warts." Such identifications are common and often informative. Here is how they work: In a nontheoretical way I already do know what warts are. They are unsightly little protuberant growths on the skin, common in adolescence, sometimes lasting for years, appearing and disappearing without warning. Only this kind of antecedent familiarity puts me in a position in which I can profit from the theoretical identification. The word "theoretical" here need only mark the contrast between what the hearer knows and what he does not know and then finds out. It need not imply that an articulated scientific or philosophical theory comes into play, or that there is an element of dubious hypothesis in the identification. Many identifications that fit this pattern are patently true and involve very little in the rôle of theory. Other examples are "Sponges are animals," "Stars are massive hot bodies like the sun," and "Lightning is an electrical discharge." In each case, when such identities are informative, the nontheoretical left side refers to something that is already known in the sense of being familiar to, though imperfectly understood by, the hearer who finds the identification informative. The main point to be borne in mind from this preliminary consideration of theoretical identifications is that one must already know, in one sense, what the phenomenon to be identified *is* if a theoretical identification is to be intelligible, much less instructive.

Identifications of mental things by philosophers of mind are commonly intended to fit this pattern. Suppose a materialist philosopher is explaining his view to a beginning class of philosophy students. By way of illustration he tells his students that visual experiences are brain events. He supposes that the students already know what visual experiences are, in one sense, but they do not appreciate that those things with which they are already familiar are actually brain events. This preliminary familiarity with visual experiences is presupposed by all philosophers, materialist or not, who propose to identify them in any way whatever. In this discussion I raise doubts about this presupposed preliminary familiarity with visual experiences.

2. Visual experience and sensuous description

The first thing to note about visual experiences is that it seems hard to describe them. For example, the materialist J.J.C. Smart once said that experiences can only be *derivatively described*.[1] Smart's derivative descriptions are not really descriptions at all, but only specifications of the circumstances under which experiences are usually undergone. More recently, Thomas Nagel, reacting to the same difficulty, said that we lack a means for conveying objectively the subjective character of experiences.[2] Perhaps we can agree that visual experiences elude ordinary descriptions, but this feature of them, if indescribability can be called a feature of them, is important to my concerns, so I will take a moment over it.

I said that the materialist supposes that others already know what it is that he is identifying with brain events when he says, "Visual experiences are identical with brain events." Though we have trouble describing visual experiences, there are some nondescriptive things that can be said about them with security. For one thing, visual experiences are supposed to be things with which people are familiar as a consequence of the fact that they can see. Blind people do not have the right antecedent familiarity, so a different example of mental things would be better for a class of blind students. Furthermore, visual experiences, although familiar in connection with sight, are not supposed to be familiar because people can see *them*. I put this awkwardly as a remark about the source of our presumed familiarity with visual experiences. We do not see them. That is not how we are familiar with them. I cannot say flatly that visual experiences are not supposed to be visible things at all, because the identification that the mind-brain theory proposes seems to imply that they might be visible. Visual experiences might be seen, for example, under magnification during brain surgery. I can say flatly, however, that whether or not visual experiences are in principle visible things, our presumed familiarity with them is certainly not supposed to consist in seeing them. And, of course, visual experiences are not familiar because we have perceived them in any other sensory modality. So none of the vocabulary that we can apply to things because we can perceive them can be applied to visual experiences. Let us sum up this obvious point by using the old term "sensuous." Our familiarity with visual experiences is not familiarity with things we can describe in sensuous terms.

Years ago the pioneer mind-brain theorist U.T. Place labeled failure to respect the nonsensuous character of experiences "the phenomenological fallacy."[3] This is the blunder of thinking that experiences, as candidates for assignment to some metaphysical status, are things that fit sensuous descriptions. The fallacy is committed by anyone who objects that materialism cannot be right since the brain cannot be the locus of the colored and noisy things we know in perceptual experience. Such an objector fails to notice that a visual experience of a yellow lemon is not a yellow visual experience, or a yellow anything. Thus, in asserting that such an experience is actually something in the brain a philosopher does not assert that there is something yellow inside the perceiver's head. Because they are not perceived and, therefore, not to be described in terms of any perceivable features, it is hard to describe visual experiences at all.

There is a second point to be made about visual experiences insofar as they are supposed to be things with which beginning philosophy students, for example, can be presumed familiar. The second point is that the nature of visual experiences has been under discussion for a long time. The mind-brain theorist believes that he is not initiating a discussion of visual experiences. He is contributing to an existing discussion. He thinks that he is now, at last, making the right identification of things that have been discussed and wrongly identified by other philosophers. In this spirit Smart says,

> Our talk about immediate experience is itself neutral between materialism and dualism. It reports our internal goings-on as like or unlike what internally goes on in typical situations, but the dualist would construe these goings-on as goings-on in an immaterial substance, whereas the materialist would construe these goings-on as taking place inside our skulls.[4]

Talk about immediate experience is, therefore, "topic neutral" as Smart and other philosophers following him in this conception say,[5] meaning that it is a way of referring to experiences without prejudice as to the ultimate determination of their metaphysical standing. We are to understand, then, that earlier philosophers, perhaps such as Descartes and Hume, considered visual experiences. Descartes, Hume, and their like identified visual experiences with ongoing nonphysical events, but Smart himself and other mind-brain theorists are offering a corrected identification *of the same inner things* with which beginning students are familiar and which Descartes and Hume misidentified in earlier philosophical efforts.

Now we have before us two ideas about visual experiences. The first is that visual experiences are not colored or otherwise sensuously describable things, and the second is that these visual experiences that are now identified by materialists are the same as those previously, and perhaps erroneously, identified by dualists. I have stated these ideas fully because they are not compatible with one another. I want to use the conflict of these ideas to help to introduce my opinion that our presumed familiarity with visual experiences is not a reliable foundation on which to erect theories which give them a theoretical identification.

These two ideas are incompatible because the inner things that are supposed to be familiar to all of us in connection with vision, the inner things that dualists have spoken of and identified, are definitely supposed to be things that *are* sensuously describable. The thing that Descartes identifies as something mental when he has the experience of seeing something yellow is something yellow in his mind, and Hume's *perishing impressions*, like the twentieth-century dualists' *sense data*, are mental things that fit sensuous descriptions. It is hard to be confident about any absolutely general claim here, but I think it will be conceded that most of these philosophers, including contemporaries such as Frank Jackson,[6] accept some version of the theory of secondary qualities according to which the exhaustive locus of application of sensuous terms is ideas in the mind, or inner representations, or sense data. Many of these philosophers think that the outer world is describable only in the nonsensuous language of mathematical science. This is an old and perhaps exhausted tradition, Jackson's current work notwithstanding. I am not endorsing it. I do want to remind us of what the inner is supposed to be like for dualists.

To think of the inner thing that is supposed to be identified as a colored thing is, for the materialist philosopher of mind, to commit the phenomenological fallacy. But the familiar things dualists are talking about are familiar colored things. So Smart's contention that we have on hand a concept of immediate experiences that is neutral between materialism and dualism is mistaken. Materialists are not merely contributing a new identification to things previously identified by dualists. Smart expressly endorses Place's remonstrance concerning the phenomenological fallacy, and he states clearly that he is not talking about things that can be colored when he speaks of immediate experiences.[7] But then he cannot be speaking about the same thing that dualists speak about. His view does not differ from theirs only in the metaphysical identification of ongoing events conceived in the same neutral way at the pretheoretical level.

What accounts for this? I say it is a manifestation of the fact that our supposedly pretheoretical notion of visual experiences is itself an unstable philosophical idea in which various strands of thought are inattentively mixed together. The idea of visual experiences is not at all what it is supposed to be, that is, simply a way of referring to what every sighted man knows about as plainly and as intimately as he knows about his shoes and socks. Smart's view seems to me to rely upon misplaced confidence in this pretheoretical notion. It is as though we say to ourselves that everyone who can see has visual experiences all the time. Just because there does not seem to be any conceivable problem about that, we do not feel the need to pin down this concept any further before getting to work with identifications. We know that materialists and dualists are men first and philosophers second. Their experiences are surely like everyone else's experiences, and surely like one another's. So we readily assume that they must be talking about the same familiar things that must be everyday matters to all sighted beings. Differences in philosophical theory are something we are ready for here, but we assume without question that we start from a common conception of the items for which a philosophical theory seems to be required. Apparently this assumption fails.

The presupposed everyday conception of visual experiences as inner things requiring some theoretical identification or other is not independent of the philosophical theories that presume to identify such inner things. The dualist's theory of secondary qualities removes sensuous features from the outer world and assigns them to the mind. The supposedly familiar things that dualists identify as mental things are actually familiar outer things that have been relocated in the course of philosophical argument. The beginning student is indeed familiar with the visible things around him. Arguments that culminate in the theory of secondary qualities, arguments which are developed before the problem of metaphysical identification is faced, persuade the beginning student and his teacher that these things are familiar, alright, but that they cannot be outer things. Thus we reach the dualist's conception of inner mental bearers of sensuous qualities.

In a second round of philosophical reflection undertaken by materialist thinkers these inner realities become nonsensuous and merely derivatively describable things. As Smart himself states, they are supposed to be the very same inner things that dualist argument has already generated. But further consideration (like Place's presentation of the phenomenological fallacy) now desensualizes these inner things, while continuing to rely upon their purported familiarity. "Of course," the materialist urges plausibly, "when you have an experience of a colored thing, the experience is not colored." Here a nonsensuous subject matter has been brought into play, while we still seem to be talking about what everyone is intimately acquainted with. If we were really acquainted with a certain nonsensuous inner reality, how hard it would be to understand that we might commit the phenomenological fallacy. How could we be so dull or inattentive as to describe as "yellow" something with which we have maximal familiarity and something which is not a sensuous thing at all? This would be much as though we tended to think fallaciously that four is a yellow number every time we were confronted with four yellow things. It seems to me that the irrepressible impulse to sensuous description in describing experiences actually manifests the fact that we have no clear preliminary idea about the inner in perception at all, so that all our descriptions naturally gravitate to the sensuous things, the outer things, that perception does, in fact, make familiar to us.

If we have no definite preanalytic idea to go with the philosophers' ideas about inner visual experiences, is it possible that there are no such things at all? The big problem with this "identification," and maybe it is the only problem, is that it sounds cranky and perverse. "There are no visual experiences" sounds cranky because sighted people obviously have visual experiences. This *is* a pretheoretical truth that does not depend on any special philosophical stand. But we do not have to move from "People who can see have visual experiences" to "People who can see are familiar with something inner when they do see." Vigorous debate about the metaphysical status of inner experiences serves primarily to distract our attention from the rôle that is supposed to be played by allegedly familiar inner things in our understanding of perceptual consciousness.

3. Thomas Nagel on subjective phenomenology

These thoughts about the inner in perception are reinforced by Thomas Nagel's discussion of subjectivity and the experience of bats.[8] Nagel argues that even if we knew everything that there is to be known about the physiology of bats, and even if we knew just which neural events in bats were identical with the bat's sonar experiences (supposing mind-brain identity to be correct), we would still not know what it is like to have such experiences. We do know that it must be like something to have a bat's experiences, that is, to occupy what Nagel calls the bat's "point of view." We know this because we have experiences ourselves. A philosophical bat wondering what it is like to have our visual experiences would be wondering about something which we know about. We humans know what our visual experiences are like, but we lack descriptions of them that could convey anything to those who do not have such experiences themselves. For Nagel mind-brain identity may be correct, but it does not shed any light on subjectivity because it leaves unaddressed the question "What is it like to have such and such experiences?" and/or the question "What is it like to have such and such things go on in one's brain?"

Nagel presents this point as a residual point for an otherwise successful materialist philosophy of mind. It seems to me that it really shows the irrelevance of the allocation of inner things to one or another metaphysical status. Nagel's thinking retains its full force if we apply it to a dualist account of experience. We could say to a dualist,

> Even if you were able to prove that conscious experiences are events in nonphysical substances, and even if you demonstrated that a bat's experiences are modifications of the mind-stuff in bats, you would not advance our understanding of subjective conscious experiences. What it is like to have the experiences of a bat would be as elusive after your demonstration as before.

Like Smart, Nagel does think that there are inner things that call for an identification. These are supposed to be nonsensuous things for reasons much like those given by Smart and Place,[9] and Nagel thinks too that they may turn out to be brain events. Moreover, when he discusses the elusiveness of subjectivity, Nagel shows the same vacillation about the character of visual experiences that Smart revealed in saying both that such experiences are nonsensuous and that they are the same inner things that dualists have previously identified.

Nagel says that we lack a language in which to frame objective phenomenological descriptions. I think that, like Smart, he means that we can say "the visual experience you get when you see a yellow lemon," but that this means nothing to a person who does not know from his own experience *what you do get* when viewing a yellow lemon. Nagel thinks, and he admits that this is just a speculation, that we might be able to develop an objective phenomenological language. We would develop the right thing if it gave us the means to convey to another creature the subjective character of experiences of a type that that creature itself does not have. Using such a language, a talking bat could let us know what it is like to have sonar perceptual experiences of the sort that the bat enjoys. At a more modest level we could explain to blind persons what a visual experience is like if we had some resources for objective phenomenological description.

Nagel suggests two directions in which we might look for this objective phenomenology. He mentions what he calls "intermodal analogies" such as "red is like the sound of a trumpet," and he dismisses this source of potential communication with the blind. Second, he says that structural features of different kinds of perceptual experience might be exploited. I have the same reaction to both of these speculative suggestions, but I will only discuss the first one, even though Nagel himself dismisses it as worth little or nothing. What is interesting to me, and what reveals Nagel's vacillation on the character of visual experiences, is his reason for rejecting intermodal analogies as a foundation for communication of the character of visual experiences to the blind. "Red is like the sound of a trumpet" is no good, because, as everyone knows, red is not much like the sound of a trumpet. In other words, Nagel thinks that the comparison of sound and color seems apt because it is the sort of thing one might be tempted to say in trying to get something across to a blind person, but the particular remark won't get anything across because of the lack of similarity.

In fact, this speculative reasoning of Nagel's betrays the instability of the preliminary idea of visual experiences with which Nagel is operating. For the illustration actually compares sensuous objects. In the context of Nagel's commitment to the nonsensuous character of the experience itself, "Red is like the sound of a trumpet" should be dismissed as irrelevant to subjective phenomenology. If red were, *per impossibile*, very like the sound of a trumpet, we would be able to tell a blind person about red things via the comparison. But we would not be talking about either visual or auditory experiences. We would be talking about things you can see and hear. Experiences are neither noisy nor colored, as Place reminded us. Being red or sounding like a trumpet are not ways that subjective experiences can resemble one another or fail to resemble one another. Are we to think that if red were quite a lot like the sound of a trumpet, then the nonsensuous visual experience of red things would be sure to be quite a lot like the nonsensuous auditory experience of trumpet sounds? I do not think this precarious hypothesis lies behind the seeming aptness of "Red is like the sound of a trumpet."

A much more convincing explanation of the appeal of the analogy is available. We want to convey something to the blind man about what he misses because he is blind. We think at once that he will not know what colored things are like, for he has never seen anything colored. The trumpet sound is obviously suggested with the thought that the blind man knows what that is like, and to those who are familiar with both, the trumpet sound seems vaguely like the color. As Nagel says, it is a very weak similarity. But the point is that although Nagel tried to think about the supposed nonsensuous inner experience, he immediately slipped back to the concept of sensuous outer objects of perception. Nagel understandably thought that an assertion that did convey what a red object is like would communicate the desired information to a creature who could fully understand the assertion, although he had never seen a red object. This is natural because perception really does make the sensuous properties of things familiar to those who are able to perceive them. But officially Nagel is supposed to be looking for a way of communicating the character of nonsensuous experiences to people who do not have them. He is not supposed to be trying to communicate the sensuous character of perceived objects to those who do not perceive them. His substitution of the second project for the first is intelligible as a product of the standard philosophical moves concerning perception that we rehearsed above. As perceivers we are familiar with the perceivable features of things around us. Philosophers initially internalize these familiar things, yielding the dualist conception of inner sensuous objects. Then the inner is desensualized again by being embedded in phrases like "the experience of seeing something red" or "the hearing of trumpet sound."[10] All the while we continue to rely on the thought that these are just the ordinary things with which all perceivers are familiar. In an unguarded moment we are apt to revert to the sensuous (because that is what is really familiar in perception), and thus we philosophers commit the phenomenological fallacy. This is what has happened in Nagel's discussion of intermodal analogies.

What is it that a blind man misses? He is not acquainted with anything you can see, for he cannot see, that is, he is not acquainted with visible sensuously describable objects. Is not that all there is to it? Or should we say that the blind all suffer a further deprivation? They also know nothing of certain inner ongoing events with elusive subjective features that are, in any case, nonsensuous and are possibly brain events. I do not think that one has to be a cranky philosopher to question this concept. The naturalness of the error of presenting a comparison of sensuous outer objects as if it were a comparison of alleged nonsensuous inner experiences seems to me to help to show the insecurity of the very idea of these inner things.

Let us turn to the larger point that Nagel makes: the essence of subjective experience eludes the mind-brain identity theory. I say that it also eludes philosophers who make other identifications of inner experiences. This is a strong point, because it seems that philosophers have always thought that our efforts at a metaphysical identification of the mental were addressed to the question of the essence of subjective conscious experience. Nagel is pointing out the fact that an identification of mental phenomena cannot provide the understanding of mental things whose need motivates the identification. Is not this message clear in much-discussed questions of the analogy between mind-brain identity and theoretical identities considered by the sciences?

The mind-brain materialist thinks and asserts that his hypotheses are something like "Lightning is an electrical discharge." Accepting this identification, those dramatic flashes and those bolts that split great trees become intelligible phenomena. Thus we do get to know what these formerly puzzling things really are. How devastating it would be if we could say of *that* identification, "Well, maybe so, but that misses the essential character of lightning." If such physical identifications are true, they do not miss the essence of what they identify. I am quite sure that those who feel the pull of a materialist philosophy of mind are responding to the hope that the mystery of consciousness can be dispelled via materialism. This is the hope that, as Herbert

Feigl put it many years ago, materialism will not leave "nomological danglers."[11] To say, as Nagel does, that the essence of subjectivity is bound to elude a materialist identification is to say that these materialist hopes will be disappointed. In the same spirit, the dualist inspiration has always been to provide a metaphysical identification of the inner that is potent enough to make conscious experience intelligible. The nonphysical mind with its moral, religious, and supernatural associations has plainly seemed fitting for the extreme puzzle of conscious experience. I think that Nagel shows that dualism imports all of these mysterious associations into the philosophy of mind to no purpose, since the identification of experiences with any metaphysical underpinning will leave the essence of subjective consciousness unillumined.

A curious echo of this theme is to be found in Davidson's concept of *anomolous monism* as a philosophy of mind. Davidson abandons hope for psychophysical laws and, therefore, accepts the irreducibility of mentalist vocabulary in the characerization of mental states. Davidson's monism is, of course, materialism, but the anomolousness is equivalent to renunciation of the Feigl-Smart aspiration of elimination of "danglers." Even though mental states are all physical states according to Davidson, our best characterizations of them will leave them unconnected with the body of physical science.[12]

4. Kripke against mind-brain identity

I am suggesting that the failure of all proposed identifications of a realm of subject matter indicates a need to revise our conception of that subject matter. If we can see that all identifications of "visual experiences" will fail equally, we might reasonably entertain the conclusion that there is something amiss with the idea of visual experiences. As long as we think we are choosing between alternative identifications, one of which may be right, we can retain the notion of inner items of some kind that need a theoretical identification. But when we recognize that all such identifications would leave us with the same questions that we thought we were resolving, then we will be ready to consider the possibility that this subject matter is a kind of conceptual illusion and not an irreducible object of acquaintance. To reinforce this picture I want to consider the views of Saul Kripke about mind-brain identity theory.

Kripke and Nagel have a lot in common. Kripke too says that mind-brain identity claims inevitably miss the essence of what they are trying to identify. But he takes that fact in itself as a conclusive ground for rejecting the identifications, while Nagel thinks that the identifications may be true even though they fail to throw any light on the subjective character of experiences.

Kripke says that theoretical identity statements such as "Visual experiences are brain events" have to be necessary truths, if they are truths at all. This follows from the fact that the expressions that flank the "are" (that is, the expression of identity) are both what Kripke calls "rigid designators." Some theoretical identifications are true. For example, "Heat is molecular motion" is presumably true, and the designators here are both rigid, so this is a necessary identity, although philosophers have commonly misunderstood such cases and called them instances of "contingent identity." Kripke shows us how philosophers managed to make the mistake of thinking that "heat is molecular motion" is contingent, and how we can straighten out the errors of that view and accept such statements as necessary truths which are known only a posteriori. But Kripke explains that, in our thinking about mind-brain identifications, we will not be able to represent them as necessary truths, which they must be if they are true at all. Therefore, such identities are false.

Kripke's critique of mind-brain identity and his conception of rigid designation on which the critique relies are controversial. I will say a few things about the inadequacy of attempted replies to Kripke's analysis, but I do not try to present a fundamental examination of this controversy. I want to express how things look in the philosphy of mind if we accept the general view that Kripke put forward. My own conviction is that Kripke's views here will survive criticism on the whole and that though his outlook may be altered and developed, there is in Kripke's thinking on this issue a solid core of permanent contribution to our understanding of things, a contribution that does not risk complete refutation and rejection. Furthermore, it seems to me that the critical views about the concept of visual experiences that we have been developing so far in connection with the opinions of Smart, Place, and Nagel fit in very well with the claims that Kripke makes from the viewpoint of modal logic and ontology.

In *Naming and Necessity* Kripke presents his critique as a kind of technical obstacle that has been overlooked by materialists.[13] In what follows I try to show that Kripke's critical remarks do not indicate an obstacle to any philosophical view that we should otherwise want to adopt. On the contrary, Kripke's results are just what one would expect and want as a consequence of an attentive examination of materialism and dualism as efforts at the identification of visual experiences.

To understand Kripke's arguments, just four points must be grasped: (i) What is the difference between a rigid and a nonrigid designator? (ii) Why must an identity using two rigid designators be a necessary truth? (iii) How is it that some necessary identities can be discovered to be true and can seem to be contingent? and (iv) Why is it that mind-brain identities could not *turn out* to be necessary, just as other identifications that seemed to be contingent truths to philosophers have turned out to be necessary and true in light of Kripke's analysis?

(i) The referring expression "heat" is a rigid designator. The expression "what causes sensations of heat in us" is like the expression "heat" in that it too refers to heat, but it is not a rigid designator. "What causes sensations of heat in us" is nonrigid in that something other than heat might have caused in us the sensations that heat actually does cause. In the jargon of possible worlds, in another possible world what causes sensations of heat in us is some other phenomenon and not heat. In contrast, if in a given possible world other than the actual world there is heat at all, it has to be what heat is and cannot be something else. Heat in another possible world has to be what heat is in this world. If we could "wake up" one morning in another possible world, and we were able to raise the question "Does the phenomenon, heat, exist in this world?" we could only answer affirmatively if we find a phenomenon in that world which is what heat is in the actual world. So "heat" is rigid, and "what causes sensations of heat in us" is not rigid.

Consider just the referring phrase "sensations of heat." This is a rigid designator. We cannot suppose that sensations of heat exist in another possible world but that sensations of heat are, for example, sensations of dampness in that other world. Of course, sensations of heat do not have to exist in every possible world, and they do not have to be called "sensations of heat" in worlds in which they do exist. In order to exist at all in another world, however, sensations of heat do have to be sensations that we would call "sensations of heat" in this world. So rigid designators pick out the same things in every possible world in which they pick out anything, while nonrigid designators pick out different things in different possible worlds. Further illustrations of which we will make use are these: Like "heat" and "sensations of heat" the expressions "molecular motions," "visual experiences," and "brain events" are all rigid designators. In contrast, the expression "what goes on in me when there is a yellow lemon, the light is daylight, my eyes are open, and so on" is like the expression "what causes sensations of heat in us." Both of these are nonrigid. Generally, applying Kripke's distinctions to the terminology we have been discussing, topic-neutral derivative descriptions are all nonrigid designators.

(ii) Given this distinction, it follows at once that an identity stated with the help of two rigid designators expresses a necessary truth if it expresses a truth. We said that rigid designators designate the same thing in all possible worlds, so if two rigid designators designate one and the same thing in one possible world, namely, the actual world, then they do so in all possible worlds. Identity in all possible worlds is just necessary identity in the rhetoric of possible worlds.

(iii) That heat is molecular motion is something that we found out. It has a contingent flavor strong enough to make materialist philosophers use this as a paradigm contingent identity to which it is hoped by materialists that mind-brain identities might be assimilated. Kripke first overthrows the claim of contingency, and then he explains the appearance of contingency. The illusion depends on the fact that we rely on a nonrigid designator to, as he says, *fix the reference* of "heat." Our fundamental way of appreciating the presence of heat is via the sensations it causes in us.* So we can use the expression "what causes

---

*One of the unresolved difficulties in Kripke's analysis of identifications arises in connection with appeals to sensations in contexts like this. For one thing, it is not clear that scientists investigating the nature of heat actually did employ the potential for producing the sensations in us in a reference fixing procedure in connection with their investigations. Furthermore, it is not clear in Kripke's discussions whether and how we are supposed to know if scientists have made use of this kind of reference fixer or have not. Again, it is not clear what difference this would make in Kripke's thinking or whether, perhaps, he thinks that, in some general way, this kind of reference fixing *must* have been employed. Perhaps more important, Kripke's appeal to sensations here may be generally questioned. Can we not suppose that a person holding a loaf of bread fresh from the oven feels the heat of the bread and is not obliged to recognize the presence of that phenomenon through the presence of a sensation, or through anything at all short of the phenomenon itself? If we agree that heat is itself apprehended perceptually, how should we restate Kripke's analysis? Or can it be restated at all?

sensations of heat in us" as a reference-fixer for "heat." Then we are in a position to discover that the phenomenon which, as it happens, causes sensations of heat in us *is* molecular motion. It is not a necessary truth that molecular motion produces just those sensations. We might have had those sensations in the absence of molecular motions, and the motions might have existed without us and our sensations. But that the phenomenon which as a matter of contingent fact does cause sensations of heat in us, namely, the phenomenon heat, is molecular motion is necessary. Being molecular motion is the essence of that phenomenon. It could not exist without molecular motion because, as the true identity says, it *is* molecular motion. Kripke says,

> In the case of the apparent possibility that molecular motion might have existed without heat, what seemed really possible was that molecular motion should have existed without being felt as heat.[14]

Thus it never really seemed possible that the phenomenon of heat might have existed and yet not have been what heat *is*. The illusion of possibility comes from the real possibility that we might have had sensations of heat in the absence of any heat, and we might have had no such sensations though heat was a present. These things would happen if heat did not produce those sensations and something else did. In that odd world heat would still be what heat is in our world and in all possible worlds in which heat exists. The possibilities afforded by the contingently related sensations of heat make epistemological room for the discovery that what produces those sensations, that is, heat, is molecular motion. In this sense we are able to discover something that is necessarily true.

(iv) Mind-brain identities proposed by materialist philosophers of mind also appear to be contingent identities. But in this case Kripke shows that the appearance of contingency cannot be explained away. The trouble is that there are no contingently related things that we can think of as our means for determining the presence of mental things. The mental events composing our conscious lives do not make themselves known to us in a way analogous to the way in which molecular motions produce sensations of heat in us. Therefore, we have no nonrigid designators for things such as visual experiences with which we can fix the reference of "visual experiences" by exploiting a contingent evidential relationship like that between sensations of heat and heat.

In the case of molecular motion and heat there is something, namely, the sensation of heat, which is intermediary between the external phenomenon and the observer. In the mental-physical case, no such intermediary is possible since here the physical phenomenon is supposed to be identical with the internal phenomenon itself. Someone can be in the same epistemic situation as he would be if there were heat, even in the absence of heat, simply by feeling the sensation of heat. . . . No such possibility exists in the case of mental phenomena.[15]

Applied to our subject matter, to be in the same epistemic situation as one would be in if one had a visual experience is to have a visual experience. Nothing else will do. That is Kripke's view.

I will consider some of the things that have been urged against Kripke's arguments. None of these responses seem to be at all satisfactory, but consideration of them does help to secure our grasp of the central issues.

Michael Levin has urged against Kripke that there are nonrigid designators available in the context of mental phenomena and that the contingent relationships expressible with the help of these available reference fixers do provide just the setting for mind-brain identities that Kripke says cannot be provided.[16] The reference-fixing nonrigid designators that are supposed to do this job, according to Levin, are none other than the topic-neutral derivative descriptions that we have discussed. Anticipating this appeal, I have listed "what goes on in me when there is a yellow lemon, etc.," as a nonrigid designator that contrasts with the rigid designator "the visual experience of seeing a yellow lemon." Now I want to show that, on close inspection, this plausible sounding challenge to Kripke's analysis does not work out.

We want to compare two identity claims: (A) Heat is molecular motion and (B) Visual experiences of seeing yellow lemons are brain events. To resolve the tricky-sounding issues, we have to expound the two cases in pedantically parallel fashion. In each case there are two rigid designators that appear in the identity statement and, therefore, refer to the same thing if the identity statement is true. In each case there is one nonrigid designator that is supposed to fix the reference of the first rigid designator. In both cases the availability of this nonrigid designator is alleged to explain an illusion of contingency in the identity statement. Thus we have two rigid designators

(A-1) heat,
(A-2) molecular motion,

and the contingent reference-fixer for "heat"

(A-3) what causes sensations of heat in us,

and, for visual experiences Levin's critique depends on these three: the two rigid designators

(B-1) visual experiences of seeing a yellow lemon,
(B-2) brain events (of some specification),

and the contingently related reference-fixer for (B-1)

(B-3) what goes on in me when there is a yellow lemon, my eyes are open, etc.

In its context (A-3) is effective in explaining the appearance of contingency not merely because it provides a nonrigid designator for "heat." (A-3)'s effectiveness relies on the further fact that we can intelligibly use it to fix the reference of (A-1). We are acquainted with sensations of heat, and we fix the reference of "heat" by appealing to the causal relationship: heat is what causes these sensations.

For Levin's analogy (B-3) must be a nonrigid designator, and we must be able to construe (B-3) as enabling us to fix the reference of (B-1). Levin is surely attracted by the following common ground in the two contexts: That (B-3) is nonrigid is assured by the contingency of the causal relationship to which it alludes. In another possible world lemons do not cause in us the occurrences that they do cause in this world. This corresponds to the thought that in another possible world heat does not cause sensations of heat, so that (A-3) is nonrigid. We must also note, however, a significant difference between the cases (A) and (B). The common referent of (A-1, 2, and 3) is heat, which is the cause in the causal relation mentioned in (A-3): "What causes sensations of heat in us." But (B-1, 2, and 3) all refer to the effect mentioned in (B-3): "What goes on in me, or is caused in me, when there is a yellow lemon, etc." In the heat context we use the effect as an epistemic mark of the cause. Kripke says, "we identify heat and are able to sense it by the fact that it produces in us a sensation of heat.[17]

What about (B)? If, in the manner of a powerful and familiar empiricist tradition, we thought we might use our perceptual experiences as the epistemic foundation for claims to know the presence of outer objects, then we would be using the effect (what goes on in us) as an epistemic mark of the cause (the lemon) just as in (A). But this possible epistemic ordering could only conceivably pave the way for a theoretical identification of lemons. On this ordering we would be using "what causes this ongoing event in us" as a reference fixer for "lemons," and only seemingly contingent identifications of lemons could be cleared up by adverting to this reference-fixing procedure.

A true parallel relevant to the theoretical identification of visual experiences must cast the presence of a lemon in the rôle of epistemic mark for the occurrence of a visual experience. Only if we could use the presence of a lemon, on the pattern of (A-3) as a way of appreciating the presence of the phenomenon to be identified, could we complete the analogy and explain away the appearance of contingency in the identity "visual experiences are brain events." But we cannot use lemons as evidence for the occurrence of visual experiences of seeing lemons. We can say, with some plausibility at least, that our way of knowing that heat is present is by noting the occurrence of sensations of heat. But we cannot say that our way of knowing that we have a visual experience is by noting the presence of the visible thing that engenders that experience.

Remember that even Smart refers to the phenomenon that he says is derivatively describable as "immediate experience." "Immediate" is a clear reminder of the fact that we do not use anything else as a guide to the occurrence of our experiences. We can imagine an occasion for saying to someone else, "You must be having the experience; the lemon is right in front of your nose in broad daylight!" But this is only rhetoric in the face of suspected untruthfulness. The person to whom the remark is addressed is not being urged to consider the presence of the lemon as a reason for thinking that he is having the right experience. And we could never use the presence of a lemon as our own contingent evidence for the claim that we are having the experience of seeing a lemon. If that were possible at all, the contingency of the relationship would mean that it could fail. A case of the failed relationship in the context of (A-3) is entirely plausible. It would be a case of sensations of heat in the absence of heat.

For a parallel in the context of (B-3) we would have to find a yellow lemon present in the absence of the visual experience. And this would not mean that there might be a lemon which we do not see. It would have to mean that we do detect the lemon as usual, but that we have no visual experience. We all understand well enough the old empiricist doctrine that we use our visual experience as evidence for the presence of outer objects. An analogous rôle for (B-3) is absurd because it requires the converse procedure. So the appearance of contingency of identities such as "Visual experiences are brain events" cannot be eliminated by the use of topic-neutral reference-fixers. Therefore, Kripke's argument against the mind-brain theory is not overthrown.

I said that Nagel's point, the subjective eludes materialist identifications, can be generalized. The subjective eludes all identifications of experiences. The very same generalization applies to the criticism that Kripke directs especially to the materialist identification of mental things. Kripke's argument has the same force and merit against any theoretical identification of mental things. However we complete "Visual experiences are . . . " so as to assert a theoretical identification, the identification will seem to be contingent and will have to be discovered. But Kripke's arguments show us that no nonrigid designator can play the desired rôle here in explaining how an identity which is necessary if true can be discovered and can appear to be contingent. If this argument is sound, it will overthrow the theoretical identification, whatever that identification is. If this is so, Kripke's conclusion ought to be the rejection of the common assumption about things such as visual experiences from which we began our discussion. This includes the assumption that visual experiences are inner items that call for some identification or other.

The generalized conclusion which I say Kripke's argument justifies is that no theoretical identifications of visual experiences are true. Since we introduced the notion of theoretical identifications very casually in the first part of this study, we do need a more detailed and careful characterization.

Some of the examples Kripke treats are not strictly identities at all. This is especially noticeable in the context of Kripke's arguments against materialist identification of mental things. The popular analogies to which materialists appeal in claiming the plausibility of the "contingent identity" of mental and neural events, analogies such as "Lightning is an electrical discharge" and "Heat is the motion of molecules," are not identity statements, or, to say the least, they do not seem to be identity statements. Were "Lightning is an electrical discharge" an identity statement, it would be an assertion of a type-identity. But such a statement would be false, since there are obviously instances of the type, electrical discharge, which are not instances of lightning. Although all bolts of lightning are electrical discharges, the converse of this assertion is false. The same holds for "Heat is the motion of molecules," although this may be somewhat obscure.

This is a serious matter because the main features of Kripke's analysis rely on the thought that we are speaking of identities. For example, if we thought that being an electrical discharge is merely a property of all instances of lightning, the theoretical identification loses its status as an identity, and the whole analysis Kripke presents becomes inapplicable. The proposition "Every S has the property P" does not have to be a necessary truth even if "S" and "P" are both rigid.[18] Thus "Cats are carnivorous" is only contingent, even if "cats" and "carnivorous" are both rigid, as they presumably are. There might have been noncarnivorous cats, although, as a matter of fact, there are not. If the property is an *essential property* of all the things to which it is attributed in a proposition, then that proposition is a necessary truth. This is part of what it means to say that a property is an essential property. But the theory of rigid designation does not serve as an explication of the necessity of attributions of essential properties, as it does for the necessity of identities. From this it follows that insofar as our intuitions are to be guided by the power of the concepts of rigidity and nonrigidity, the identifications under discussion must be thought of as identities.

In other words, since "Lightning is an electrical discharge" and "Heat is the motion of molecules" are not identity statements as they stand, we must substitute other statements for these which capture the spirit of Kripke's analysis and which are identity statements. There are obvious ways in which this might be done. For example, as long as we explicitly reject the idea that being an electrical discharge is a property of phenomena and insist that electrical discharges comprise a type of phenomena, we will be entitled to say that the type lightning is identical to a subtype of the type: electrical discharge, that is, precisely the subtype consisting of discharges of electricity which are instances of lightning.

The availability of this type-identity statement is, in fact, guaranteed by the truth of the nonidentical proposition "All instances of lightning are instances of discharge of electricity." The substitutable type-identity is obtained via what traditional logicians called conversion by limitation. This effort to provide a clear identity statement raises complex issues and does not by itself reinstate Kripke's analysis, even though the identity of instances of lightning with a subclass of electrical discharges is indisputable. To bring the substitute identity statement within the scope of Kripke's thinking, we have to be able to say that both referring terms that appear in the statement are rigid designators. But the very fact that we must rely on conversion by limitation for assurance that there is an underlying identity indicates that there is no natural language designator at all, apart from "lightning," for the limited class of electrical discharges that are discovered to be cases of lightning. Since we have no designator for this class of electrical discharges at all, we do not have a rigid designator and cannot state the identity in a formula where two rigid designators flank the expression for identity. This issue and the question of other possible routes by which Kripke's thinking may find application to such cases go far beyond the scope of this study, and I cannot predict the outcome of them with any confidence. In spite of this, it seems that the analysis Kripke offers will be sure to fit the identifications materialists imagine that neuroscientists will be able to assert in the future.

The hopes of the mind-brain materialist would be fulfilled if we were to find a perfect correlation between events fitting a specific description in mentalist terminology and events fitting a specific description in physical terminology and were then able to promote the correlation statement to an identity statement. This aspiration itself includes the thought that scientists will not be left with the mere inclusion of a certain kind of mental phenomena within a larger class of physically described phenomena, which is what creates the problem in the case of the so-called identity of lightning and electrical discharge, and of heat with the motion of molecules. Richard Rorty's fantasy identifications bring out this intention of the materialists.[19] Rorty uses an intentionally simplistic schema of firings of neural fibers which are identified by a code of letters and numbers yielding identities such as

> Remembering that mammoths are extinct is the firing of M 491.[20]

There are no obvious problems standing in the way of interpreting this kind of formulation as an identity stated with two rigid designators.

Therefore, the technical problems that beset "Lightning is an electrical discharge" and "Heat is molecular motion" will not impinge on the mind-brain identifications which materialists envision. These will be straightforward identities stated with two rigid designators, and Kripke's arguments will apply with full force to them.

Kripke's critique of materialism is addressed primarily to what is called "type-identity" theory.[21] Types, like sets, properties, numbers, and propositions are abstract entities. So, the visual experience of seeing a yellow lemon is a type, as is the firing of neuron E 125 (exploiting the spirit of Rorty's imagined realization of materialist identifications). Particular experiences, such as Sally's visual experience of a yellow lemon at time t, are tokens of the type, visual experiences of seeing a yellow lemon; and the firing of neuron E 125 in Sally's brain that begins at t is a token of the type: neuron E 125 firing. Some materialists propose "token-identity" theories, and they say that criticisms of type-identity do not apply to token-identity versions of materialism. What do they have in mind?

Let us consider the type-token issue in the setting of our fundamental interests and expectations in the philosophy of mind. Our attention is attracted to mental things such as perception, belief, memory, sensation, and so on. There seems to be a range of phenomena here whose nature we do not understand. Of course, we have in mind actual particular events such as Sally's visual experience and Tom's headache. We want to know what these tokens actually are. Is Sally's experience at t identical with the firing of neuron E 125 in Sally's brain at t? Is Tom's headache actually identical with C-fiber activity in Tom's brain during the period of his suffering? Or do these identifications fail for some reason? It looks as if we are interested in identifying tokens from the outset. We want to know whether token mental events are identical with token physical events in token brains at particular times.

In a way it seems inevitable that we should be interested in the character of token mental events, since most philosophers and others who think about it will surely suppose that token mental events comprise all the mental events that there are, have been, or will ever be. Thus, insofar as we are interested in the nature and metaphysical standing of mental events, it is token mental events in which we are interested, since all mental events are token mental events.

Perhaps some will object to this ontological parsimony on one ground or another. Are there not, in addition to the mental events that ever exist, further possible mental events? Let us say that there are, without investigation of the question. I am emphasizing only the thought that these mental events that are not events in the actual world are possible *token* mental events such as beliefs and pains that Sally and Tom never have at any time, but beliefs and pains they might have had at some time or other. In agreeing that pains which do not exist are nonetheless possible we are not committing ourselves to mental subject matter which, were it to be found in the actual world, would not consist in token mental events but in something else. Nonactual but possible mental events are all token mental events.

The same holds for scientific projects that attempt and presumably succeed in identifying flashes of lightning or instances of the phenomenon heat. It is tokens, that is, actual flashes at particular locales and times, and actual heat that is here and now somewhere and at some time, that attract our scientific curiosity. The thought of possible bolts of lightning that do not occur, and of heat that might have existed, is the thought of the possibility of tokens of lightning and heat.

Where do types come in? If a type such as the visual experience of a yellow lemon is an abstract object, and we are permissive about the *existence* of abstract objects and the existence of this one in particular (whatever it means to be permissive about this), then we think that this and other abstract objects exist *in addition to* concrete objects such as token experiences and token brain events. But the materialist philosophy of mind, whether of the type-identity or token-identity variety, does not propose to identify abstract objects in addition to its identification of concrete tokens. The assertion that the type, visual experience of a yellow lemon, is identical with particular events in particular brains is as unintelligible as is the claim that the armchair in which I am presently seated might be discovered to be an abstract object.

There is nothing mysterious about the fact that type-identity theory does not identify mental types with something material, but rather, like token-identity theories, type theories identify token mental events with token physical events. I am spelling out these thoughts because they are often invoked and seldom made explicit. The idea of materialist identification of visual experiences of a yellow lemon is that all the tokens of this type are physical event-tokens of the type, neuron E 125 firing. This is a type identity in virtue of the claim that the mental and physical types collect the same individuals.

The issue of possible tokens helps to bring into focus what is really involved in the type-token distinction here. Let us suppose that all the actual tokens of type A are tokens of type B, and vice versa. The claim that such is the case can be asserted in the form of an A-B identity theory. What about a token of type A that might have existed but does not exist? Call this possible A-token, a_0. Had a_0 existed, would it have been identical with a B-token that we may designate b_0? The identity theory that asserts that an A-token must be a B-token is a type-identity theory. It asserts that it is of the essence of A-tokens to be B-tokens. This claim goes further and explains the extensional identity of the class of A-tokens and B-tokens. This advance beyond the range of actual tokens is what is involved in the difference between type-identity and token-identity theories.

Because it makes a modal claim about token identities, a type identity will support counterfactuals of the form: Had an A-token been present, it would also have been a B-token. This support of counterfactuals can be viewed as a conceptual link between type identities and scientific laws. Conversely, it is because Davidson's conception of mental events asserts that each is a physical event but renounces the hope for discovery of psychophysical laws (or even perfect correlations) that Davidson's is a token-identity theory.

It seems to me that we would expect a type-identity theory to include the theoretical understanding that explains why A's must be B's. For example, researchers might know that some symptom appears only in connection with an invading colony of bacteria of a certain kind. That does not guarantee that that bacteria is the cause of the symptom and not merely the occasion for the presence of a different cause that is introduced only with the bacteria but could, in principle, occur in other ways.

Philosophical theorists envisioning a scientifically achieved mind-brain identity often express their vision in terms of the discovery of a perfect correlation of mental and brain events, together with an appeal to Ockham's razor. They say that a discovered perfect correlation, combined with reasonable ontological restraint, ought to establish type-identity. This stand may be shared even by those who, like Donald Davidson, insist on a token-identity thesis. Davidson supposes that we have to be satisfied by token-identity because we cannot get any psychophysical laws which would be expressions of the perfect correlation. Materialist philosophers of mind neglect the fact that perfect correlation would not ordinarily be sufficient as a foundation for type identity in other scientific contexts. An explanatory account would be required before a type-identity thesis is deemed established. In place of the explanatory account philosophers insert a conviction that non-material identifications are intrinsically mysterious and hopelessly infected by association with discredited worldviews. Although we might sympathize with these attitudes, they should not be allowed to obscure the fact that the basic format of type identity is not satisfactorily replicated even in the imagined scenario of mind-brain identity. The explanation in virtue of which we can see that instances of mental events must be instances of neural events is not even envisioned by materialists when they are giving rein to unfettered fantasies about the future accomplishments of neuroscience. That is, we know what an explanation would be like that would show that the invading bacteria, and not something else, *is* the cause of some symptom. Such an explanation would provide details of the mechanisms by which the symptom is produced. But we have not any idea of what it would be like to show that a certain neural event, and not something else, *is* a visual experience. So Ockham's razor is invoked here because in this context we lack any idea of another kind of reason for advancing from correlation to identity. In my view this lack ought to be traced to inadequacies in the preliminary conception of the inner subject matter, whose elements it is supposed that philosophers of mind might try to identify.

Some critics of Kripke's arguments against mind-brain identity have urged that the materialist philosophy of mind can be defended because it is not properly expressed in identity statements wherein rigid designators flank the identity sign. Thus Richard Boyd proposes an interpretation of materialism which makes it into the claim that mental events are essentially physical without entailing any thesis of the form "Rigid designator$_1$ = Rigid designator$_2$."[22] I have already conceded that an identification of mental phenomena that amounts to an attribution of an essential property is not susceptible to Kripke's criticisms, and Boyd's thinking fits this characterization. Boyd raises many issues which cannot be pursued here. It is worth noting, however, that in order to present this interpretation of materialism, Boyd finds it necessary to describe Kripke's initial intuitions in a way that is by no means uncontroversial and is, in fact, inadequate, in my view. Thus Boyd says,

Kripke's claim that the standard strategy contingent identity fails for statements that follow from a materialist account of mental phenomena rests on the (very plausible) claim that certain mental states have as essential properties the way they feel.[23]

If this were a satisfactory representation, the whole theory of rigid designation would not find application to the issue of materialist philosophy of mind for the reason that attributions of properties, essential or otherwise, are not identity statements at all, so that the necessity of identities has no implications for such statements. Kripke takes it that pains are feelings of a certain kind, not that pains are phenomena that have as a property (essential or otherwise) that they feel a certain way.

Quite apart from Boyd's analysis, the resources of metaphysical redescription sometimes seem to solve problems or avoid them by a kind of magic. The use of the concept of properties is like this. At the outset we think of the concept of properties as a concept that contrasts with that of individuals, which are the things that have or lack properties. It is identities of individuals that give rise to Kripke's analysis. But of any individual, b_0, we can always create the property of being b_0, and then we can restate the identity

$$a_0 = b_0$$

as the nonidentity statement

a_0 has the essential property of being b_0.

If we begin from the intuition that difficulties flow from the identification of mental events with brain events, we should not be persuaded to abandon those intuitions by the availability of a way of speaking that conceals the identity claim by reassessing it in terms of the attribution of a special and essential property.

The solution or avoidance of problems about metaphysical identity through the expedient of an always-available redescription in terms of properties of phenomena is a sleight of hand that can deceive even its own practitioners. This move is akin to the nominalization of "I see a red, white, and blue flag," yielding "My seeing of a red, white, and blue flag," which magically absolves identity theorists from finding anything red, white, and blue in accounting for the realities with which visual perception apprizes perceivers.

5. Whether there are any visual experiences

There are some "identity statements" about visual experiences which are certainly true and others which seem to me to be true. "Visual experiences are visual experiences" is true, and so too, I believe, are "Visual experiences are experiences you get when you see things" and "Visual experiences are the conscious components of visual perception."[24] If we accept these assertions, I think it will help us to understand what is at stake in Kripke's critique of the materialist philosophy of mind. They help because these identifications have no flavor of contingency. No one will think of these as formulating scientific discoveries or philosophical hypotheses about visual perception. We can mark the difference by introducing "really" in theoretical identities, that is, in identities which can seem to be discoveries or philosophically interesting claims. The word "really" captures both the necessity of theoretical identities and their seeming contingency. "Really" gets at the necessity and essential character of an identity in that it carries the force "nothing but" or "none other than." "A is nothing but B" conveys the inevitable necessity of identities between rigidly designated phenomena, but "really" can also carry the sense "contrary to widespread opinion" or "surprisingly enough," and this expresses the a posteriori element and the appearance of contingency in theoretical identities. A true identity that does not function as a theoretical identity will not accept "really" with grace. Consider "Visual experiences are *really* the conscious elements of visual perception" or "Visual experiences are *really* the experiences you get when you see things." "Really" has no job to perform here. It conveys nothing and sounds idle and out of place. That is simply because there is no theoretical identity asserted and no seeming contingency.

In the philosophy of mind our metaphysical interest in visual experiences amounts to a curiosity as to what they really are. Like other mental things, visual experiences threaten to be an unwanted burden to our ontology. But Kripke's argument against mind-brain identity is actually an argument against any identification of visual experiences whatever. Any theoretical identity claim, and not just the materialist's claim, will have to be necessary if it is true. Any such identification will seem to be a discovery that lets us know at last what the nature of these conscious events is. The appearance of contingency will have to be explained away for any such identification. Such an explanation will always require a nonrigid designator to function as a contingent reference-fixer. It is always the discovered identity of what this reference-fixer happens to refer to that creates the atmosphere of contingency in the identity claim. The rôle of such a reference-fixer will be just the same no matter what identification of visual experiences is made. It will have to be an epistemic mark of the presence of what we are about to identify. If nothing can be used as such a mark for the presence of conscious experiences, an explanation for the apparent contingency of a theoretical identification of those experiences will always be lacking. Then the identification will be false, whatever it happens to be.

This argument for the generalized conclusion is just the same as Kripke's argument for the rejection of the mind-brain theory. There can be no intermediary to play the rôle that sensations of heat play in the context of "heat is molecular motion." If we could say that visual experiences characteristically cause something else in us, call it Y, then we could set up the identity "What causes Y in us is (really) certain brain events." If Y could also figure in the right epistemic rôle, we could think of visual experiences as whatever it is that produces Y in us. Then neurologists might show us that visual experiences are brain events, and the case would be just like "heat is molecular motion." (Strictly, the case would be better than that of "Heat is the motion of molecules" in that the theoretical identification of visual experiences would be expressed in a true identity statement, as remarked above.) Any other theoretical identification of visual experiences, such as the dualist identification "Visual experiences are modifications of nonmaterial constituents of perceivers," would rely on exactly the same preliminary reference-fixing in terms of Y. The need for this has nothing at all to do with what identification might turn out to be correct. The contingent reference-fixer is required in order to make sense of the question "What are these things identical with?" But Kripke purports to show, and I think no one has sustained another view, that there can be no such contingent reference-fixer Y. So every attempted theoretical identification will lack footing in just the same way, and, therefore, every such identification will be false.

To recapitulate, we cannot use anything but the mental state itself as an indication of the presence of the mental state. It could not be that in the actual world we rightly think that we have a certain mental state, such as a particular visual experience, because Y is pres-

ent, and concede that in another world we might use the presence of
Y as the epistemic mark of a different experience. Therefore, nothing
can play the rôle of a contingently associated epistemic mark of the
presence of a visual experience. All theoretical identifications of the
form "Visual experiences are . . ." fail.

In discussing the inaccessibility of bat experiences Nagel says that
we have to face the possibility that there may be things that we can
never find out about.[25] Is that our situation here in view of the failure
of identifications of visual experiences? We will never be able to
establish an identity for them. We will never find out what visual experiences really are. Plainly, this is not a good way of putting our situation relative to visual experiences if Kripke's understandings are correct. This *ignorabimus* would be apt if we could never find out which
of all possible alternative theoretical identifications of visual experiences
is the true one. But armed with Kripke's insights, we know that all
of them are false. Literally we could put this by saying, "Visual experiences are not really anything." There will be no answer to the question of what these puzzling things really are. They do not have any
metaphysical standing as this or that kind of event. There is nothing
to know about such things that we do not already know.

In the philosophy of mind we are inclined to say that there are
certain inner things that go on when we perceive. I have claimed in
section (2) of this chapter that our conception of these inner things
is itself a product of philosophical pressures and the ideas that we
develop in response to them. These inner goings-on are not the neutrally
conceived, philosophically innocent phenomena Smart tried to invoke.
We seem to be committed to such inner things by the theory of secondary qualities and other dualist and materialist ideas we have mentioned
in our discussion, and also by complex reflections about perceptual
aberrations and by philosophical interpretations of the known physiology of perception. Surely there are also common sense and everyday
habits of thought and speech that seem to suggest or even to require
an inner object of perceptual consciousness. As materialists we find
that there is nothing that we can offer as a straightforward descriptive
account of these inner things. We have to use derivative descriptions,
and the search for an adequate phenomenological language has yielded
nothing so far. Now to this somewhat discouraging picture of indescribable inner experiences we have to add the further pessimistic
thought that identifications of them are not just permanently unsettled.

They are all definitely false. At the very least this conclusion shows us that we are certainly wrong in thinking ourselves and our beginning students as antecedently familiar with visual experiences which will have to be identified in one way or another. We are not entitled to the starting point of investigators trying to identify a phenomenon because we already know that any proposed identification will be false.

I think we should simply give up the thought that in the philosophy of mind we are faced with familiar phenomena standing in need of identification. Kripke's argument may help us to overcome the sense that the repudiation of inner things is a perverse philosophical stance. This could be expected if, as I urge, what we have been treating as an intuitive datum all along is in fact the product of expendable philosophical argument. If this is so, it seems to me that we may one day raise to the level of a formidable intuition the idea that visual perception only acquaints us with visible things in the world that we can see and describe, and that visual perception does not acquaint us with any inner phenomenon at all.

NOTES

1. See J.J.C. Smart, "Materialism," *J. Phil.*, LX, 1963; as reprinted in C.V. Borst, editor, *The Mind-Brain Identity Theory*, London, 1972, p. 162.
2. See Thomas Nagel, "What Is It Like to Be a Bat?" *Phil. Review*, LXXXIII, 1974 pp. 435-50.
3. See U.T. Place, "Is Consciousness a Brain Process?" *Br. J. of Psych.*, LXVIII, 1956; as reprinted in Borst, *The Mind-Brain Identity Theory.*, p. 48. Note that Place discusses this "fallacy" in connection with the dualism of Sir Charles Sherrington. The transition from the prephilosophical notion to Sherrington's dualism, and from the latter to Place's materialism, illustrates the historical development of the concept of experiences that I describe in this section.
4. Smart, "Materialism," p. 162.
5. Smart introduced this Rylean epithet into discussions of materialist philosophy of mind in "Materialism," p. 164. An important example of the acceptance of Smart's characterization of experiences in the formulation of the identity theory is D. Lewis, "An Argument for the Identity Theory," *J. Phil.*, LXIII, 1966, pp. 17-25.
6. See Frank Jackson, *Perception*, Cambridge, 1977, ch. 5.
7. Smart, "Materialism," p. 161.

8. Nagel, "What Is It Like to Be a Bat?"

9. See Nagel, "Physicalism," *Phil. R.*, LXXIV, 1965; as reprinted in Borst, *The Mind-Brain Identity Theory*, especially section 2, pp. 215-19.

10. Nagel himself attains such desensualized subject matter for identification by philosophers of mind by embedding the operative descriptive terminology in phrases such as "my having a sense impression of . . . ," "Physicalism," p. 217.

11. See Herbert Feigl, "The Mental and the Physical," *Minnesota Studies in the Phil. of Sci.*, Minneapolis, vol. II, 1958, p. 428. Smart makes use of the claim to avoid nomological danglers in "Materialism," cited above, and elsewhere.

12. See Davidson's "Mental Events" in L. Foster and J.W. Swanson, editors, *Experience and Theory*, Boston, Massachusetts, 1970; reprinted in Davidson, *Essays on Actions and Events*, New York, 1980.

13. S. Kripke, "Naming and Necessity," in D. Davidson and G. Harman, editors, *Semantics of Natural Language*, Dordrecht, Holland, 1971; revised edition, S. Kripke, *Naming and Necessity*, Cambridge, Mass., 1980.

14. Kripke, *Naming and Necessity*, p. 151.

15. Ibid., pp. 151-52.

16. See Michael Levin, "Kripke's Arguments Against the Identity Theory," *J. Phil.*, LXXII, 1975, pp. 149-67; and *Metaphysics and the Mind-Body Problem*, Oxford, 1979, pp. 113-27.

17. Kripke, *Naming and Necessity*, p. 131.

18. This was pointed out to me by Joseph Almog.

19. See the chapter "The Antipodeans," in Richard Rorty, *Philosophy and the Mirror of Nature*, Princeton, New Jersey, 1979.

20. The illustration is based on an example Rorty himself gives. Sometimes Rorty writes as though his view should be thought to be a version of eliminative materialism rather than mind-brain identity. Whatever the ultimate character of his own position on the nature of the mental, Rorty's explicitness on the provision of a physical event-type imagined to be identical with a mental event-type is representative of the standard expectations of the mind-brain identity theorists.

21. See Kripke, *Naming and Necessity*, pp. 144-45.

22. See Richard Boyd, "Materialism without Reductionism: What Physicalism Does Not Entail," in N. Block editor, *Readings in the Philosophy of Psychology*, vol. I, pp. 67-106, esp. pp. 85-87.

23. Ibid., p. 82.

24. For a similar point see H. Putnam, "The Nature of Mental States," in D. Rosenthal, editor, *Materialism and the Mind-Body Problem*, Englewood Cliffs, New Jersey, 1971, p. 151.

25. Nagel, "What Is It Like to Be a Bat?" p. 441.

VI

Action and Teleology

If, as Melden claims, causal explanations are "wholly irrelevant to the understanding we seek" of human actions then we are without an analysis of the "because" in "he did it because . . . ," where we go on to name a reason.

Donald Davidson[1]

Whether or not actions are caused, reason-giving explanations do not appeal to the causes of the actions they explain. This once-popular view has been challenged, most notably by Davidson in the essay quoted above. In this chapter I will contend against views like that of Davidson and for a noncausal interpretation of reason-giving.

I will consider first teleological explanation of events that are not actions. Such explanations provide a nonmysterious paradigm for explanations of occurrences that do not consist in picking out causes for what is explained. I do not know whether to say that just this much is a controversial claim. In any case, the character of teleological explanations will be examined here with a view to securing agreement on the general proposition that a teleological explanation of phenomena in an organic system or a machine makes essential reference to the effect of the event explained and does not refer to causes. Correct teleological explanations can be given in cases where the causes of what is explained are unknown.

The further point of this discussion is the application of the concept of teleological explanation to the context of reason-giving explanation for actions. I mean to provide an analysis of the "because" in "he did it because . . ." that Davidson finds wanting. Many reason-giving explanations fall under the general pattern of teleological explanation and are, as such, not to be interpreted causally. I do not claim to have shown that all reason-giving explanations are teleological. Reason-giving is not a precise concept. Those explanations that Davidson called "rationalizations," the explanations for which he said that "primary reasons" can be given, appear to fit the pattern of teleological explanation quite readily.

1. The standard view of ends, ends-in-view, and causality

A provisional idea of the thesis to be defended here can be had by focusing on the rôle of reference to the objectives or goals of actions in reason-giving explanations. One line of thought is so commonly followed that it deserves to be called the *standard view*. Suppose a man explains his action as contributing to some future state of affairs. The standard view regards this as a condensed account wherein what is really intended is the assertion that, prior to acting, the agent had reaching that state of affairs as an objective, or that prior to acting he intended to reach that goal, or desired to reach it, or had reaching the objective as an end-in-view. What I call the standard view depends on the intuitive feeling that if we fail to convert a reference to a future state into a reference to a prior aim, we will wind up explaining the present in terms of the future. This would be an unacceptable finalism that violates the temporal direction of causality and affronts firm convictions about nature. When we have deleted reference to the goal in favor of reference to *having that goal*, we have moved from the temporal framework later than the action to the temporal framework earlier than and up to the action. This prepares us to entertain the question Could this item "His having such and such an objective" be thought to have caused a man's action?

Much of the discussion of action and causality in the last few decades has been focused by following this standard line of thought. We are brought to think of having an intention, of wanting to accomplish something, or of setting an objective as event-like items. We are to regard them as occurrences in the mental life of the agent. The debate centers on the appropriateness of thinking of these alleged prior occurrences as causes of what reason-giving explanations explain. Familiar debates have hinged on the conceptual independence that is required of causes and effects. Can intentions or desires be individuated without essential reference to the actions they are supposed to explain? This kind of question becomes relevant only if we accept the move from outcome to aim.

The standard line about reason-giving tends to make conscious functions a prominent element in the understanding of action. Our reason-giving abilities rely on matters such as planning, thinking about what will happen under various circumstances, realizing that particular steps will bring about a particular situation, consciously making an effort, and conceiving of one's situation and prospects in a specific and articulated way. These conscious activities play a rôle in the standard line of thought about action because one can and one often does think about what one will do prior to acting, and one can decide to try to attain a goal before acting on that decision. Familiar prior conscious activities, therefore, provide illustrations that appear to encourage the view that it is always possible to restate reference to outcomes in terms that substitute prior ends-in-view, so that there is always an element in a reason-giving explanation about which the question "But isn't this the cause?" is apt.

In what follows I concede that these conscious functions are connected with the *giving* of explanations of one's own actions but are not a part of the *substance* of such explanations. The fact that a man can think in advance that he will act to attain a certain goal is another manifestation of the fact that he is able to say, having acted, what the goal of his action was, that is, to what outcome it contributed. When a man thinks over things and forms an intention before acting, he knows what he will do, and *he knows why*. He projects his action together with a teleological explanation for it. The fact that he knows the explanation in advance does not convert it into a causal explanation.

The standard view induces a double shift in focus in philosophical discussion of reason-giving explanation. The first shift is from one temporal frame to another. If we accept this shift, we agree to consider matters that might, at any rate, be causes of what is explained in that they belong to the temporal frame appropriate for causes. The particular matters to which attention is directed are then such things as desires, intentions, decisions, and beliefs. So the second shift moves us from the question of the temporality of explanatory matters adduced in reason-giving to the question of the causal efficacy of mental things. The standard view thereby trades the problem of finalism for the quandries of mind-body interaction.

Teleological explanation of organic and machine phenomena is unencumbered by the concept of consciousness. This is a great advantage for philosophical analysis. Isolation from unresolved issues in the philosophy of mind makes it possible to clarify a concept of explanation in terms of outcomes that is not causal explanation. When we have a good grasp of this concept, we are in a position to see the force of reason-giving explanations without being distracted by issues relating to consciousness. If we accept the view that I advance here, we are still entitled to the question "How is it that men are able to give reasons for their actions?" I do not treat this important question here but rather try to distinguish it from the question "What does a man say about his action when he gives a reason for having performed it?"

2. Teleology and compensation

I call any explanation that derives its explanatory force from appeal to the outcome, goal, or objective of what is explained a teleological explanation. In physiological contexts where there is no question of intentions, desires, or beliefs the validity of this type of explanation seems to be intuitively evident, although this appearance is often undermined by philosophical reflection and criticism. In the absence of subtleties it seems obvious that some teleological explanations are true and others false. It is true to say that sweating occurs to cool the body and false to say that pumping it to the brain occurs to cool the blood. Teleological explanations can have different kinds of objects. Regularities are explained (sweating when it is hot), as are particular events (a rise in the rate of perspiration of an individual on an occasion) and the possession of organs (sweat glands). To further the analogy with explanations of particular actions, I will consider only teleological explanations of particular occurrences. Within this restricted domain I will not present an analysis that tries to fit all cases but will confine attention to a single kind of illustration, namely, teleological explanation of instances of compensatory activity.

Any study of the human body reveals many compensatory physiological activities; among them (and most useful for our purpose) are instances of homeostasis, of which the maintenance of stable body temperature is an often-discussed example. I choose this illustration because it makes it particularly easy to separate the single issue of the outcome-orientation of explanations from other questions with which this single issue is often mixed up. The concept of compensation gets its footing from facts like these: Things happen in the environment of the human body that would, of themselves, cause significant changes in internal body temperature, but body temperature does not change much. Temperature stability is maintained in the face of destabilizing causal factors. How does this happen?

Although the full physiological story involves complex neural functions and is, as far as I know, not yet fully understood, there is no mystery here. Threats to the stability of body temperature are accompanied by offsetting changes in the body, such as changes in the rate of perspiration. Sweat on the skin evaporates and causes heat loss. The more sweat, the more heat loss. Perspiration is only one of the physiological resources for temperature control. Blood vessels dilate and contract. Various glands secrete various amounts of various substances. Under normal conditions, with the mediation of neural functions, perspiration together with other physiological responses combine to produce a joint causal influence that is precisely suited to the maintenance of stable temperature under the particular environmental conditions that happen to present themselves.

Homeostasis makes the fact of compensation obvious because environmental challenges and physiological responses can be extremely varied, whereas the outcome — stable temperature — remains the same. What is obvious is that a body reacts *in whatever way is required under the circumstances so as to produce the same outcome* vis-à-vis body temperature. To deny that this is what happens would be to suppose that the constancy of the outcome is somehow an accident or a coincidence. Such a denial would entail a refusal to predict that a given threat to stability will be accompanied by just the needed offsetting changes. The willingness to make that prediction, in turn, is equivalent to the acceptance of the idea of compensation. No one takes seriously the thought that the constant outcome might be an accident or coincidence, and everyone would predict offsetting changes to stability threats. Hence, it is right to say that the physiological changes do, indeed, compensate for environmental changes that would affect stability. The body is so structured that it produces whatever response is needed to secure the stability of internal temperature. The stability of the outcome is the foundation of our predictions and explanations of compensating activities.

This account is oversimplified in a number of ways. Some environmental changes are not offset. If it becomes too hot, temperature stability within the body will be lost. Some possible environmental temperatures, such as 1,000,000° F, are so great that they would destroy not only temperature stability but also the very circumstances under which talk of internal temperature is meaningful. But where we can speak of compensation, there is a range of environmental changes for which compensation does succeed. Again, there are important differences among cases in which a given outcome is not preserved. Fevers sometimes have their own teleological explanation: to eliminate a heat-sensitive, invading micro-organism. But fever can also result from the failure of temperature control mechanisms. The detailed structures required for these distinctions are complex but do not introduce anything that challenges the concept of compensation. The same is true of the fact that temperature-controlling responses of the body may compensate not only for environmental threats to temperature stability but also for changes originating within the body itself.

The concept of the outcome preserved by compensating changes may be more or less arbitrarily specified. Three outcomes with respect to which human bodies manifest compensatory activities are these:

O_1: Body temperature in the range 98.1-99.1° F.
O_2: Body temperature in the range 98.0-100.0° F.
O_3: Body temperature in the range 90.0-100.0° F.

The degree of compensatory success ascribed to an organism will depend upon the choice of outcome and the range of environmental change for which that outcome is preserved. In actual investigations of organic systems we think of outcomes preserved by compensation in terms of the normal functioning, health, and survival of organisms. Then outcomes are easily thought of as goals related to the welfare of the system manifesting compensation. These understandings do not play any part in the concept of compensation and outcome-oriented explanations *per se*. We could readily identify compensatory behavior whether or not we possess any understanding at all of the outcome preserved and whether or not the preservation of that outcome does contribute anything whatever to the welfare of individuals or species. This point will be significant in discussions to come.

3. Compensation and causality

In physiological illustrations of compensation the event that compensates for environmental changes is a causal factor for the outcome adduced in a teleological explanation. That it will maintain normal temperature explains a change in perspiration rate, and that change, under the circumstances, causes the temperature to fall in the normal range. So the explanatory factor is the effect of the explained event. Teleological explanation would be finalistic if it represented the outcome as, somehow, the cause of the changes that produce it. But there is no reason to make such an implausible claim. The outcome is the effect in the ordinary sense and temporal order of things, but it is the effect that is explanatory. This is not at all, as is sometimes suggested, simply a way of bringing out the thought that the cause is a necessary condition for the effect. It is the compensatory structure of the behavior of the system generally that supports the teleological explanation, and not merely the fact that causes are necessary for their effects. It is only because we believe that just the right compensating change needed to cause *this* effect will be the one that occurs that we say of one such change that it occurs in order that the outcome be attained.

Causality bears on the concept of compensation at a second critical juncture. This fact can prompt skepticism about the distinctive character of teleological explanation. We have said that where compensation exists, environmental changes are accompanied by offsetting changes so as to bring about a given outcome. This accompaniment is itself a manifestation of causal relations. Let S be a system that reveals compensatory activity with respect to an outcome O, let F be a particular environmental change that threatens the attainment of O, and let E be the instance of compensatory activity that offsets F and, under the circumstances, causes O. What accounts for the fortunate occurrence of E just when F comes along and threatens the maintenance of the outcome O? No doubt the occurrence of E is a consequence of a causal link between F and E. In other words, F threatens O and at the same time causes E, which removes the threat, again causally. A teleologically organized system is precisely one that works in a way that guarantees that this will happen for a range of environmental changes. There will be causal explanations for everything that happens in such compensatory mechanisms. Does teleology then reduce to causal explanation? I say that it does not.

Engineers are called upon to construct machines that exhibit compensatory activity, and that means activity that will be teleologically explicable. In building such a machine an engineer has to exploit causal relationships between the machine, its environment, and possible outcomes. He is not called upon to go beyond such causal relationships or to build in an occult device that anticipates the future. Outcome-oriented explanation is a feature of events in it because of the organization of his machine, given its environment, and not a further component or peculiar principle operating in it. It is for just this reason that teleological explanation in terms of compensation and outcome-orientation can be both successful and nonmysterious.

We can say that a fully understood compensating change is a causal link between an environmental change and the outcome. F causes E, which causes O. It would be entirely misleading, however, to say that the explanatory force of a teleological explanation comes from a tacit reference to the causes of the event explained. On the contrary, confidence that there is a causal relation between F and E is frequently engendered by acceptance of the teleological explanation itself. Our ideas about the causal history of a teleologically explained event may have no support at all apart from the teleological explanation. We recognize that E compensates for F because E-like responses to F-like threats *actually do attain O.*

The example of homeostasis makes this particularly obvious. This much puts us in the position to assert, "Since E offsets F so that O is attained, there must be a causal connection between F and E, for we do not think that the compensatory activity is a miracle." In actual biological investigations the discovery of homeostatic phenomena and other end-oriented organization raises the question of the causal relations that underlie compensation. Compensation can be identified and teleological explanations rightly given whether or not we have discovered anything about the causal history of the compensating events.

This point is brought out with special force when the demand for teleological explanation includes some causal understanding of the puzzling event: "Why does working in hot weather make us sweat?" This is answered by: "To keep the body temperature from rising." The only causes of E (sweating) that we are familiar with are already incorporated in the explanation-seeking question. Surely they cannot also be presented as the answer. Here we are thinking of explanation for the layman. The conceptual point remains the same in the context of a technical explanation for E. We might know all there is to know about the cause of E but not know the teleological explanation for it. Teleological and causal explanations are independent. When we eat, enzymes are released in the saliva to trigger the secretion of hydrochloric acid in the stomach and facilitate digestion. Who knows

what causes the release of enzymes? Experts surely have a causal account, and we could learn it. After reaching a complete causal understanding of E, we might discover that the teleological explanation was
wrong to begin with. The enzymes may not be what causes secretion
of the acid. Then, too, the expert explanation we accept for E may
prove to be wrong without threatening the teleological explanation.

4. Teleology and behaviorism

I mean to use the pattern of teleological explanation considered
so far as a paradigm for explanations of actions that state reasons for
which they were done. A teleological explanation is never restatable
as a causal explanation. Reference to an effect or outcome of what is
explained is the crux of teleology. The standard view of reason-giving
insists on a preliminary shift from outcomes to aims on the ground
that appeals to outcomes are finalistic, if they are not heuristic short-
hand for appeal to causes. The cases we have examined show that, as
a general thesis, this is not true. There are plenty of correct explanations that advert to outcomes and not to causes. I plan to show that
many reason-giving explanations of actions fit this pattern, so that the
preliminary shift is quite without justification.

In his book *Teleology* Andrew Woodfield follows a line of thinking that is as opposed to what I will argue as is possible.[2] Whereas I
argue that nonmentalistic teleological explanations of events that are
not actions should be our model for reason-giving, Woodfield argues
that mentalistic reason-giving explanations of actions should be our
model for all teleological explanation. Woodfield's position is much
influenced by his criticism of "the theory of goal-directedness" or of
"directive correlation" that was developed by G. Sommerhof, E. Nagel,
and others.[3] These accounts of teleology, like my own, which is much
indebted to them, try to explicate teleological organization and teleological explanation without introducing anything either finalistic or
mental in the contexts where teleological explanations have footing.

According to Woodfield's critique these efforts to dispel mysteries
employ a spurious conception of goals and goal-directedness, and
this vitiates their account of teleology. He finds the theories of goal-
directedness excessively *behavioristic*. Wherever explanations that invoke goals are legitimate, Woodfield contends, we must be able to

say who it is that has the goal, and we must be able to posit an inner state that constitutes *the having of that goal* by the organism. This, in turn, means that we must be able to think in terms of desirelike and belieflike states or events in organisms that have goals.[4] At least Woodfield believes that all this is essential to the core concept of teleology from which usage has been extended more or less figuratively to other contexts that resemble but fall short of core cases. In other words, Woodfield accepts the standard view of the reconstruction of reason-giving explanations of actions, and then he extends that conception to teleological explanations generally. Apparently, even in contexts like temperature homeostasis, Woodfield will insist on one of three alternatives: (a) a posited framework of mental states and events, (b) an analogical similarity to cases where mental states and events are posited, or (c) the rejection of teleological explanations.

I cannot here try to do justice to Woodfield's very full and subtle discussions of the problems of teleology. Some of the questions he raises are matters on which I do not have a view that is satisfactory. At the same time I am quite confident that the mentalizing of all teleology is a big step in the wrong direction. I will consider only two themes here in the hope of making my antimentalism plausible. The first theme concerns the concept of a goal; the second is the claim that teleological organization and teleologically explicable behavior are manifest and, therefore, cannot be thought dependent upon posited, unobserved states.

In describing compensation and homeostasis in part 3 I intentionally avoided the expression "goal" and the expression "goal-directed behavior." I do not think that we should describe temperature stability as a goal of organisms that exhibit temperature homeostasis. This usage is worth avoiding just because it does give rise to the question "Who or what is it that has this goal?" and the question "In what does the possession of this goal by the organism consist?" When these questions go wholly unanswered, the very idea of outcome-oriented explanation comes to seem suspect. But that appearance is mostly the result of the ill-advised use of "goal" for the outcome for which compensation is exhibited in the behavior of the organism. We do not look for an owner of an outcome as we inevitably do look for the owner of a goal. So confinement to "outcome" deletes a mentalizing temptation.

We saw above that where there is compensation, the description of the outcome is arbitrary or, in any case, determined by understandings that are external to the fact of compensatory organization. Just what temperature is it that a human body maintains? There is nothing to be said against any of the three different outcomes formulated in part 3 or against other specifications. Woodfield thinks that where teleological explanation is truly apt, we ought to be able to point to something answering to the idea of "having the goal G." But is it not extremely doubtful that we should ever find a reason for identifying one of the possible temperature ranges as the goal that the organism actually has? Notice that if we make the outcome range narrow—for example, 98.5–98.7° F—we will not be able to identify changes that keep temperature within wider limits as compensatory at all because they simply fail to maintain temperature in the chosen narrow range. Obviously, many compensatory events will be excluded since normal temperature so often strays from this range. A very wide range, such as 93.6–103.6° F, is no better. Though body temperature rarely escapes it, this range does not capture compensations that offset less extreme threats. Within this huge outcome range an environmental factor that would, by itself, cause a fever of 103°F would not even count as a threat to stability!

Our decision to think of some one range as "normal temperature" does not mean that this is the range the body really cares about. For every choice of ranges, wide, narrow, or medium, there will be compensatory activity that fails to be represented as such given that choice. The recognition that a system exhibits compensation is compatible with this variability in the description of the outcome. Thus the concept of compensation does not require that any outcome be identified as the real goal of the organism.

The fact that we can sometimes explain events teleologically even though they fail to attain the designated outcome is one of the reasons for which it seems tempting to think of the outcome as a goal. A goal, as Woodfield remarks, is an intentional object, and reference to it can explain even if it is not reached. Since this is sometimes true of outcome-explanations, outcomes seem goal-like. But to speak of goals is to speak of what an agent has in mind, what he is trying to do, whether or not he succeeds. The concept of an outcome does not support these ideas. We understand that sweating is explicable as producing normal temperature, in the first instance, because it succeeds in compen-

sating for threats to normal temperature. On the basis of that understanding we will explain an instance of sweating teleologically, even
though the outcome, normal temperature, is not produced. We may
know, for example, that it would have been produced if the ambient
temperature had not been so very high.

It is this sort of consideration and not analogies with conscious
effort that accounts for teleological explanation in the face of goal-
failure. Goals may be intentional objects; outcomes are certainly not.
As Woodfield says, analysts of "goal-directedness" do not justify their
use of the word "goal." But the concepts of goals is simply not required at all for understanding compensation and, with it, teleological
explanation.

I say that compensation is manifest in the behavior of an organism.
In contrast Woodfield's requirement of an inner state of having goal
G is intended as a condition for the legitimacy of teleological explanation. In the absence of such an inner state we are supposed to withdraw
the use of teleological language or, at best, to regard it as analogically
extended usage. This is simply a mark of Woodfield's overconfidence
in the standard view that recasts outcome-oriented explanations as causal
explanations. It means, for example, that to the extent that we do not
believe that the body contains a state roughly describable as "having
the goal of keeping temperature normal," we should deny that the
body does maintain normal temperature. No one, however, is going
to deny this. Will Woodfield want to invoke unconscious mental items
here, as he suggests elsewhere?[5] Does temperature homeostasis in lower
animals go to show, as Woodfield says, that "Minds may be far *more*
widespread than some philosophers have thought?"[6]

It seems clear that whatever scruples we feel about teleological
explanations in physiology, nothing will be advanced by ascribing to
ourselves unconscious ends-in-view, desires, and beliefs to go with every
subtle manifestation of outcome orientation discovered in the body.
The blood coagulates to minimize losses through bleeding. If we accept this explanation, it will not help us to express our understanding
of the phenomenon to posit an unconscious desire to keep our blood
from flowing out. Even if I have such a desire, it will be utterly inef-
fectual in the absence of the mechanism of coagulation. And with the
mechanism of coagulation blood loss through bleeding will be limited
whether I desire it or not.

Woodfield's discussions of teleology are consistently sensitive to conceptual problems, but the direction in which he turns for solutions is faulty because of his reliance on the standard view of reason-giving as the ultimate pattern for all teleological explanation. The misuse of the word "goal" in the tradition that Woodfield calls behaviorist may be largely responsible for the inadequacies of his own thinking about teleology. Essentially he believes that where one can properly speak of goals, one must be able to speak of the having of goals; goals will inevitably be the intentional objects of desire-like states and thus impose the general format of mentality on any context where goals play a part. A behaviorist analysis like that of Nagel uses the concept of goals but makes no room whatever for any part of the required mental states or for any analogs to them. So behaviorism fails.

Woodfield is entirely right in this criticism. The proper response, however, is simply the deletion of the concept of goals from the behaviorist reconstruction of teleological explanation. We can thus retain the insight that teleological organization is something discoverable about a system and its environment that requires no behind-the-scenes functioning of any kind. As I have insisted above, compensatory structure is simply observable in behavior, and homeostasis makes this as obvious as it can be. Of course, it is correct to predict that the very organic changes that will maintain temperature stability are the ones that will occur. Compensation would be ascribable and prediction justified even if we had no idea whatever about either the utility of stable temperature for the organism or the causes of the bodily changes that ensure it.

Many philosophers reflecting on teleology have thought, "To be sure, this homeostasis is a good thing for the organism, but ought we say that changes are teleologically explicable unless we think that the organism, in some sense, wants and tries to secure homeostasis?" The fact is that compensatory behavior would authorize teleological explanation even if we could make out no advantage to the organism in the outcome and even if there were, in fact, no such advantage. Patent compensatory structure of behavior will always inspire speculations and research aimed at providing an understanding of the utility of the outcome and of the cause of the compensatory events. Recognition of the existence of compensation is in no way dependent on our actually attaining some understanding of the utility of the outcome or of the causal history of the events that we can explain teleologically.

5. Theology and evolution

Compensatory behavior motivates investigation of the causal mechanisms that make compensation possible and also motivates the question "How does the body come to possess these mechanisms?" Just as recognition of compensation does not depend on our understanding the causes of compensatory activity, so too the existence of compensation and its complete causal analysis do not depend on our success in explaining how systems exhibiting teleological organization come to exist.

Familiar theological arguments are relevant here. The body has features that are wonderfully suited to the welfare of the creature. It is as though bodies were designed as devices to secure that welfare. The body of a man, for example, is equipped with sweat glands as though its designer foresaw the need to control temperature in variable environments. Might not God be the designer here? If this were right, we could see through the phenomena to the goals and purposes of God. I am not interested in the merits of theological thinking here but rather in its assumptions concerning teleology and the goals and purposes of designers. Now that we have entered the age of genetic engineering, the format of the argument here is intelligible with or without the theology. We can plausibly discern the mentality of a designer through the structure and function of a machine made of springs and valves and gears.

There is something like the standard view at work again here in arguments that go from perceived organization to posited designer. Finding a subtly operating outcome-oriented mechanism, we look for an agent-designer to be the owner of the goals that the mechanism *automatically* attains. This way of putting the matter gives rise to the idea that the teleological discourse that comes into play rests on the mentality of the designer, and that the machine or organic body itself is only described in teleological language because it is the concrete embodiment of means to ends that are expressly desired by the designer. We can say that an automobile's carburetor exists in order to mix air with fuel only because this was the designer's reason for including a carburetor in his design. We can say that the human body maintains a constant internal temperature only because God has equipped it with sweat glands and other features so that its temperature should remain constant. This is the thought that teleology in mechanisms reduces to teleology in the goal-seeking actions of designers of them. The thought is based entirely on conflating explanations of events that occur in mechanisms with explanations of the existence of those mechanisms.

If the reduction in question here were not an error, we would be obliged to say that — in the absence of a designer — teleology in nature is only an illusion to be replaced by straightforward causal explanation. That is, we would say that if the human body was not designed by God or by anyone else, then it is not a teleologically organized system at all, but only seems to be one. In the heyday of the debate between the mechanists and vitalists I think that this principle was widely accepted by both sides. Entelechies and vital forces were like self-contained surrogates for a designer. Those who rejected these concepts and proposed a natural etiology for organisms of the sort suggested by the theory of evolution seemed to believe that the advocacy of such a view included opposition to teleological explanation in biology altogether. The hardheaded scientific school wanted to read teleology out of the organic world because science admits no designer for natural things and, therefore, no owner for any goals. Without an owner of goals there can be no goals. With no goals there can be no teleology.

I hope the appropriate refutation of this reduction of teleology to the goals of designers is by now familiar to the reader. Since compensation and teleological organization are manifest in behavior, failure to find a designer cannot possibly entail the absence of compensation and teleological organization. It is the irrevocable recognition of compensation that generates the designer argument. The pattern here is (a) *since there is compensation*, we need an explanation for this fact, and a designer would be a good explanation. The pattern is not (b) *If there is compensation*, then there must be a designer. Only from the latter would it follow that there is no compensation if there is no designer.

Abandoning the theological designer argument does nothing to cloud our perception and study of compensatory mechanisms in the body. The very existence of evolutionary explanations of the existence of compensatory mechanisms (again, independent of the correctness of those explanations) should make this evident. The main point of evolution-based explanations is that they do not posit anything in the rôle of a designer, whereas they do accept the demand for some explanation of the existence of mechanisms whose operation is patently teleological.

If this point stands, we are entitled to a further conclusion. In the case of artifact machines, where there is a designer, the outcome orientation of the structure of the behavior of the machine is conceptually independent of the thoughts, goals, and purposes of the designer. By hypothesis, a compensating mechanism in a man-made machine exists as a consequence of the purposes and foresight of designers and builders. But that they are compensating mechanisms is simply a fact about the structure of mechanisms in relation to their environment and not an allusion to the mental processes of their designers. A simple thermostat system compensates for changes in the temperature of a room by turning on and off a furnace: to say this is to remain at the level of the activity of the mechanism. Teleological explanation is fully authorized by the fact that these activities are compensatory. The system actually maintains a stable temperature. In the case of an artifact we are entitled to infer designer goals from machine performance. We are not entitled to reduce teleological explanation to appeals to the goals of the designers of systems that exhibit teleological organization.

6. Teleology and action

In "Teleological Explanation and Teleological Systems" Ernest Nagel does not address the question of the bearing of his analysis on human action and reason-giving explanation. In fact, he seems to adopt a conception of reason-giving explanation in passing that would rule out the possibility that teleological explanation might serve as a pattern for reason-giving. Although I do not follow Nagel in this connection at all, I do believe that attention to his apparent line of thought is instructive. Consider this passage:

> Quite apart from their association with the doctrine of final causes, teleological explanations are sometimes suspect in modern natural science because they are assumed to invoke purposes or ends-in-view *as causal factors* in natural processes. Purposes and *deliberate goals* admittedly play important roles in human activities; but there is no basis whatever for assuming them in the study of physico-chemical and most biological phenomena.[7]

Here Nagel is dismissing the charge that teleological explanations are anthropomorphic. (Curiously enough, Woodfield's criticism of

Nagel is roughly the claim that they ought to be anthropomorphic.) Nagel thinks teleological explanations would be anthropomorphic if they ascribed "purposes and deliberate goals" to the nonhuman phenomena they explain, but as his analysis shows, teleological explanations do not require any rôle for these concepts. In passing, Nagel makes it clear that he regards reason-giving explanations of human actions in much the same way as does Davidson. Purposes and ends-in-view are "causal factors." In its reference to ends-in-view this passage illustrates what I have called the standard line of thought. A man has an end-in-view before he acts or when he acts, so that "having an end-in-view" could be a candidate causal factor for the explained behavior. A restatement of the explanation that adduced the end or outcome rather than the end-in-view would not make this candidate cause available.

Finally, Nagel's word "deliberate" in "deliberate goals" illustrates the pattern of thinking that appeals to conscious activities as a support for construing the purposiveness of actions in terms of antecedent events in the mind. In this case the conscious activity would be the deliberate adoption of a goal or the adoption of a goal after conscious deliberation. Actually, the words "deliberate goals" are rather awkward. Why does not Nagel just say "purposes and goals"? The answer is surely that Nagel's account of teleological explanation of nonhuman organic and machine functioning will speak of "goals." He introduces "deliberate" in the context of human action out of the conviction that what is important in the human case is that people consciously think about what they are going to accomplish, weigh considerations, and so on. All this is true. If I am right, however, this is not what gives explanations of actions in terms of objectives and outcomes their force.

The prima facie case for regarding reason-giving as a kind of teleological explanation is strong. Whatever the bearing on action of the cluster of concepts—conscious deliberation, foresight, desire, understanding, planning, trying, and so on—reason-giving explanations obviously refer actions to objectives, outcomes, or end-states that are caused by the explained events. Consider an illustration of Davidson's: "I flipped the switch because I wanted to turn on the light." Ordinarily in such cases my flipping the switch certainly does cause the end-state: having the light on. Although Davidson's "I wanted to turn on the light" is perfectly natural, so too is simply "In order to turn on the light." Only the standard view of reason-giving explanation requires that the latter be considered a condensed version of the former.

The straightforward causality involved in the relationship between the switch flipping and the light going on contrasts with the murkiness of the supposed causal account of the act of flipping the switch. I say that on the surface of it it seems likely that the accessibility and intelligibility of the reason-giving explanation is a consequence of its reliance on the straightforward relationship between the act and the objective, and not on the precarious system of hypotheses converting reference to the outcome into reference to a prior state of *wanting*, together with the dark speculation that the wanting caused the relevant swtich-flipping action.

To move beyond a primitive preference for the teleological interpretation of reason-giving, two analyses are relevant: (1) The context of reason-giving and action must be shown to exhibit structural similarities to the context of teleological explanations of events that are not actions. I believe that the similarities are so full and evident that they strengthen the credentials of the teleological interpretation to such a degree that the superimposition of a further causal claim about the explained action comes to seem entirely gratuitous. Contrary to Davidson's contention we do have a convincing and natural analysis of the "because" in "He did it because . . ." that is not a causal analysis. Once we agree that the structure of a man's behavior in acting bears detailed similarities to the structure of teleologically explicable activities in organic systems and machines, it becomes very hard to avoid the conclusion that the made-to-order pattern of teleological explanation — outcome-oriented and noncausal — is just what we need in understanding the force of reason-giving.

(2) The standard line of thought must, at last, be expressly evaluated. The pull of the standard line is very strong. In construing reason-giving as teleological explanation we seem to ignore the thought that the agent may experience pangs of desire before acting, that he may think it all out consciously beforehand, foresee the consequences of his action, and deliberately set himself to realize those consequences. The resurgent standard view will insist on a rôle for these things in reason-giving explanations. Isn't it true that he only did it because he realized beforehand that . . . ? Didn't his gnawing desire finally drive him to do it? In short, the bare appeal to the attainment of an outcome seems to leave out something essential in reason-giving, however

apt it may be for cases of compensation. It isn't just that the light is caused to go on by flipping the switch that makes it appropriate and true to say, "I flipped the switch in order to turn on the lights." Reason-giving involves my recognizing such causal relations and wanting to exploit them. Defense of the teleological interpretation requires either that this appearance of inadequate attention to these ingredients is an illusion or that giving the fullest play to these ingredients is compatible with the teleological interpretation of explanation of actions.

7. Action as compensation

A satisfactory parallel between events in a teleologically organized system and actions depends upon finding something like compensation in ordinary action. The first thing to be noted on this head is that actions can be patently compensatory behavior for the maintenance of a homeostatic outcome. Given a man in a room with a thermometer, a heater, and an air conditioner, we can construct a perfect analogy for the control of body temperature where the compensating events are not the operations of automatic mechanisms but the actions of the man. A man steering a boat with the help of a compass is a naturally occurring illustration of the same type. The homeostatic outcome is the coincidence of the direction of the motion of the boat and a point of the compass. Whenever currents, swells, or wind would move the boat from the given heading, the helmsman acts so as to maintain the constant outcome-state. Here we find exactly the relationships that obtain in a physiological system with homeostatic compensatory activities, except for one point. In the exposition of physiologically based homeostasis we required that the environmental event needing to be offset be causally related to the compensating event, which is then explained teleologically as occurring in order that homeostasis be maintained.

In the context of action-based homeostasis this relationship between the outcome-threat and the compensating occurrence is uncertain. It is an action that does the compensating, and we cannot baldly assert that the helmsman's action is *caused* by the shift in the wind that tends to move the boat off course and thus threatens the heading in a manner for which the helmsman compensates. Insofar as we are in doubt about the relationship of action and causality, we cannot simply claim a causal relationship here. This uncertainty is a significant issue for the teleological interpretation of reason-giving. But uncertainty here does not tell in favor of accounts like that of Davidson.

In this kind of illustration a man's action is fitted into a context that has exactly the same broad organizational features as a teleologically explicable instance of compensation in a physiological context. We cannot draw the unqualified conclusion that reason-giving (in this kind of case, at least) is teleological explanation because the causal relationship between outcome-threats from the environment and compensatory events is essential to our account of teleology, and it is not clear that it is to be found where compensations are actions. However, if the relationship between outcome-threats and compensating actions was found to be causal, that would tell *against* a causal interpretation of reason-giving, *against* the standard view, and *against* Davidson's account. The discovery (or decision to say) that actions are caused by the events that threaten homeostasis would remove the only scruple standing in the way of saying that the helmsman with compass and boat *constitutes* a teleologically organized system and does not merely resemble such a system. It is precisely in teleological systems, where the relationship in question is certainly causal, that one can give teleological explanations that do not adduce causes of what they explain. We know that it is the heat that somehow causes sweating that offsets it and keeps temperature within the body stable. But the teleological explanation cites the outcome and not the cause of the sweating. Were we satisfied that the shifting wind somehow caused the compensating adjustment at the helm, we would be in a position to say with confidence that the explanation "He moved the wheel in order to stay on course" is teleological and not causal.

Doubts about this causal relationship are not a serious threat to the teleological interpretation of reason-giving in any case. We required a causal relationship in the case of physiological compensatory activity in order to understand how the right compensating event manages to accompany the right threat. Without a causal relation compensatory behavior would appear either miraculous or coincidental and, in that case, not really compensation at all. That is why we posit a causal connection between environmental changes and compensatory responses, though we are ignorant of the details. In the context of action, doubts about the causal character of the relation between environmental changes and compensating actions do not have the same basis at all.

We do not suspect that if a compensating action was not caused by events threatening a goal, then it is not compensation. Those who hold that actions are uncaused do not mean that actions do not help to bring about objectives. Whatever the relationship between environmental change and compensating act, that relationship will support counterfactuals such as "Had the wind not shifted as it did, the helmsman would not have done what he did." Even in the setting of physiology it is the support of counterfactuals like this and not an actual causal story that is crucial for the recognition of homeostasis. All we really need know about rises in environmental temperature and sweating is that had the environment not become hotter, the sweating would not have occurred. Compensation and teleology could be systematically characterized by substituting supporting counterfactuals for causal connection between threat and compensation. We could then distinguish two ways in which this condition could be satisfied, since both activities *caused by* threats to homeostasis and actions *prompted by* threats to homeostasis offer the needed counterfactual support.

We have considered only very special examples of explanation of actions constructed in order to create a systematic resemblance to physiological homeostasis, that is, examples wherein actions plainly compensate for outer influences for the sake of the maintenance of a constant outcome-state. Within the framework of this narrowly conceived set of examples the basis for rejecting a teleological interpretation for reason-giving explanation seems to shrink to dogmatism. But most human actions do not offer such good analogies to physiological compensatory activities. For the most part actions are not compensations prompted by the presence of some particular factor that threatens homeostasis. The difficulty, however, in seeing actions as similar to compensation stems largely from the fact that there is nothing in particular to pick out as the environmental menace to a given objective and, therefore, nothing for which the action could be viewed as compensating.

The maintenance of body temperature and the steering of a boat are both examples of homeostasis, and homeostasis puts the concept of compensation in high relief just because it draws attention to specific influences that threaten the homeostatic goal. The control mechanism is structured in relation to these influences so as to prevent their having their normal effect and thus protect the "goal." It is not the case that all organic and machine activity that is teleologically explicable is homeostatic. Enzymes are released in the saliva to bring about the secretion of hydrochloric acid, but the release of enzymes does not keep the value of some organic parameter in a constant normal range on the analogy of temperature control.

I have directed attention to homeostasis, not because it is essential to teleological explanation, but only because the constancy of the outcome makes the outcome-orientation of our explanations most obvious. For the most part actions pursue short-term goals that cannot be represented as homeostasis; however, this does not tend to show that reason-giving explanations for actions are not generally teleological.

One might say that any action that is done to bring about something or to reach some objective compensates for the fact that the ordinary course of events does not bring about that something without help. A man wants to see in a dark room. The world being what it is, the light is not going to go on by itself. So a man compensates for this general feature of the world by flipping the switch that turns it on. Looked at in this way, the compensatory character of most actions is masked by the fact that nothing usually stands to bring about the objective except the action itself, and nothing stands to impede the objective if the action is done. Action is a kind of limiting case of compensation. The action compensates for the general failure of the world to produce the objective without intervention from the agent.

Somewhat more naturally, a kind of compensatory character is detectable in the fact that circumstances sometimes do block the success of the undertaken and ordinarily effective action. Reason-giving explanations carry the implication that the failure of the explained action to reach its goal would have prompted other actions as explicit compensation for whatever obstacles it is that have prevented attainment of the objective. A man who wants a lighted room will do various things besides flipping a switch in order to turn on a light if other actions are needed. He will pull chains, test bulbs, run extension cords, check fuse boxes, and pay overdue electric bills. There is no particular limit to the things that might be relevant and that might be done. The explanation "in order to turn on the light" does not define the lengths to which a man would go rather than let this objective remain unattained. This parallels the fact that the correctness of teleological explanations outside the context of action also implies nothing about the range of variations for which the teleologically organized system will provide compensation, although it does imply that there is such a range.

Intuitively, if we accept a certain reason-giving explanation, we will certainly expect that the agent was prepared to do other things that he recognized as alternative routes to his objective, especially if those alternatives are of equal simplicity and without deterrent side effects. To establish that action is essentially compensatory, however, we have to go beyond appeal to customary expectations. We have to show that reason-giving actually carries the implication that compensatory actions would have been undertaken had the explained action failed.

The required allusion to alternatives and consequent compensatory structure is tacitly incorporated in Davidson's account of reason-giving. According to Davidson "a primary reason" always involves two elements: "a pro attitude towards actions of a certain kind" and a belief "that [the performed action] is of that kind."[8] The appeal to a class of actions of a certain kind is needed because "we cannot explain why someone did what he did simply by saying that the particular action appealed to him; we must indicate what it was in the action that appealed."[9] This leads us to a general class of actions, since any appropriate characterization of the explained action will impute to it something that other actions will also possess. Davidson shows that the particularity of the action "I turned on the light" is not shared by the pro attitude "I wanted to turn on the light." The latter does indicate a pro attitude toward a general class of actions, although grammatical similarities mask the generality:

> If I turned on the light, then I must have done it at a precise moment in a particular way — every detail is fixed. But it makes no sense to demand that my want be directed at an action performed at any one moment in some unique manner. Any one of an indefinitely large number of actions would satisfy the want, and can be considered equally eligible as its object.[10]

Davidson does not say that the members of the class of actions alluded to in a primary reason include alternative actions that would compensate for obstacles to the attainment of an objective. It is certain, however, that the principle of similarity in terms of which actions are "of a certain kind" has to be the fact that they are all thought by the agent to be ways of bringing about the objective. In the quoted passage Davidson seems to have in mind only trivial differences between actions having the same outcome, such as flipping the switch with my right index finger, flipping the switch with my left index finger, etc. This is all that is needed to show that a general class of actions is involved. But true alternative actions emerge as constitutents of the class toward the members of which the agent has a pro attitude in a further example Davidson offers: "If I say I am pulling weeds because I want a beautiful lawn, it would be fatuous to eke out the account with, 'And so I see something desirable in any action that does [make], or has a good chance of making, the lawn beautiful!' "[11] Davidson means that it would be fatuous just because this general assertion is obviously implied by the reason-giving explanation.

What is common, then, to all the actions that are equally objects of a pro attitude involved in reason-giving is that they are all causally relevant to the same outcome, namely, to the objective of the explained action. Upon reflection we are entitled to say that compensatory actions will be found in any such class of actions, even those that appear to differ only trivially. After all, if my left index finger proves to be too weak, will I not try to flip the switch with another finger, that is, if I really do want to turn on the light? In saying that the generality involved in pro attitudes is equivalent to the ascription of compensatory status to actions, I mean to assert that a man who explains performing one action by saying that it belonged to a class of actions toward each of which he had a pro attitude is, at the same time, committing himself to the assertion that had the performed action been inefficacious in attaining the goal that defines the class in question, then (in the absence of countervailing reasons) he would have performed one or more other such actions in order to secure the goal.

The number of alternatives that stand to compensate for the failure of an action may be limited, and a man can fend off challenges for failing to employ recognized alternatives rather easily, saying, for example, "I just didn't care about it that much" or "I decided not to bother." He may be ignorant of available alternatives, and he may reject otherwise viable alternatives that he does recognize for countless reasons. But reference to the limited urgency of the objective, or ignorance of alternative means to it, or countervailing reasons against their adoption are all of them pertinent only because of the general implication that alternative courses would be pursued if the one adopted did not produce the objective. Were this implication to fail utterly, were the agent to wholly reject liability for this implication, or to have no explanation at all for not satisfying it, then the reason-giving explanation would itself fail.

Thus, the concept of reason-giving explanations of actions reproduces the essential features of teleological organization that we found to account for the intelligibility of explanations that cite effects rather than causes. An explained action is referred to its objective or goal, and reason-giving explanation implies the kind of compensatory plasticity upon which the analysis of teleology was found to depend. Therefore, noncausal teleological explanation constitutes a natural interpretation for reason-giving. The premise that no noncausal interpretation of the "because" in a reason-giving explanation is available, the premise that motivates Davidson and other causal theorists, is overthrown. As Davidson himself expressed this premise, "Failing a satisfactory alternative the best argument for a [causal] scheme like Aristotle's is that it alone promises to give an account of the mysterious connection between reasons and causes."[12]

This connection is no longer mysterious. Reasons explain actions by referring them to their effects and to the compensatory character of behavior vis-à-vis those effects. In light of the availability of this interpretation there is no foundation at all for the expectation that reason-giving explanations may *also* refer to the causes of what they explain. We have seen that in connection with organic or mechanical outcome-oriented explanation the question of the causal history of teleologically explained events is always raisable. No answers to this question, however, are contained in teleological explanations themselves.

8. Pro attitudes and causality

In the interpretation of reason-giving put forward here I press for the elimination of any rôle for the fact (where it is a fact) that the agent wanted to attain the objective reference to which explains his action. Of course, I do not deny that agents commonly do want to reach the objectives that their actions do reach. The teleological interpretation removes reference to this antecedent desire in favor of reference to the outcome itself. The thesis that I called the standard view of reason-giving earlier in this essay regards antecedent desires and beliefs about their possible satisfaction as the very crux of reason-giving. Can I really mean to assert that the mere outcome of the action can be explanatory without the mental processes of the agent who desired and tried to produce that outcome? I do not assert that the mere fact

that an action has a certain outcome will validate an explanation adverting to that outcome. We must believe that the agent was disposed
to compensate at least for some obstacles had the outcome not occurred.
Action has a compensatory aspect that is entailed by reason-giving explanations but is not legible from the outcome alone.

This parallels organic cases closely. Suppose that we know about
a creature S that its environment changed in temperature from T_1 to
T_2 and that the effect of this on the constitution of S produced an
internal temperature of T_0. By itself this outcome does not vouch for
any teleological explanation. We have to know about the structure of
S and, in particular, its compensatory organization. This means that
we have to know what would have happened on other circumstances
before we can offer "in order to reach to retain T_0" as an explanation
for anything. In the same way desires and beliefs are relevant to explanations of actions because they are the source of our confidence in
the compensatory dispositions of the agent, and not because desires
and beliefs cause his actions.

It is worth emphasizing that the teleological structure of reason-
giving explanations is independent of the resolution of the question
"Do desires and beliefs cause actions?" We have seen in the setting
of organic homeostasis that compensation involves two causal relations.
The compensating event in the organism causes the homeostatic outcome (under the threatening environmental conditions), and the threatening environmental conditions cause the compensating event in the
organism. We saw that the existence of these two causal relationships
cannot be construed as implying a causal reading for teleological explanation. This is brought out by the independence of the teleological
and causal explanations of the compensating event. The causal account
may be utterly unspelled out, or may be in error and rejected, or may
be corrected, without affecting the teleological explanation at all. The
causal account may be correct, and the teleological explanation may
turn out to be mistaken (in case we are right about what causes perspiration and wrong about what perspiration causes). If we have complete
knowledge of the relationships, the causal account of the compensating
event cannot be substituted for the teleological explanation.

When we compare these relations with the context of explanations of actions, the question of the causal powers of desires and beliefs
is analogous to the question of a causal account for a compensating
event in an organic system. We said that the compensatory element

in action must support counterfactuals with the form "Had such and such obstacle arisen, the agent would have taken such and such compensatory course." The thought that desires and beliefs cause actions would show up as part of the background of the truth of such counterfactuals. Roughly, the perception of the obstacle would be presumed to engender a belief about the prospects of various courses of action. The desire together with this obstacle-appreciative belief will cause an action that compensates for the obstacle.

I do not endorse any such account of desire, belief, and causality. But that is not at issue. If this causal theory of mental items were fully acceptable, its contribution to the understanding of reason-giving explanations would be limited to the auxiliary question "What caused the compensating action?" Insofar as we see compensation in action, we cannot substitute the successful account of this auxiliary matter for the teleological explanation of action. By the same token, uncertainty, both empirical and philosophical, about the status of desires and beliefs vis-à-vis the causes of actions is no more relevant to teleological explanation offered in giving reasons than uncertainty about the causal account of sweating is relevant to the fact that sweating occurs to keep body temperature normal. In sum, whether the claim that certain desires and beliefs caused a given action turns out to be true or false, that causal explanation is not even in the running in the search for the character of objective-oriented explanations of actions.

This contention faces a formidable objection. I say that prior desires and beliefs are strictly irrelevant to reason-giving, which should be interpreted teleologically and not in terms of antecedent matters at all. The objection is the plain fact that reason-giving explanations are commonly formulated by simply stating the desires and beliefs that might or might not be causes. "Why did you flip that switch?" Natural answers will include "Because I wanted the light on" and "Because I thought that would turn the light on." The availability of these formulations undermines the credibility of the analogy of action and compensatory physiological activities. In the physiological framework "to maintain stable temperature" does not name the cause of sweating on the surface of it. In consequence it is conceivable that the teleological explanation is not an appeal to causes. But reason-giving explanations explicitly mention desires and beliefs. If these are the causes of the action explained, how can one possibly argue that the explanation that is offered by mentioning these desires and beliefs does not really invoke their causal efficacy?

Part of the difficulty here stems from the use of the verb "want" and its connection with desires. There is no denying that if I flipped the switch in order to turn on the light, it will be proper for me to say, in a sense, "I wanted to turn on the light." "He wanted to . . ." is available in the context of any action that could conceivably be explained by adverting to an outcome or objective. The formula with "want" will always be constructible out of the outcome or objective mentioned. The universal feasibility of "want" formulas is, however, misconstrued as an expression of the presence of something like a prior state of desire for the outcome. On the evidence provided by this misconstruction the causal picture of reason-giving in encouraged to regard behavior that tries to satisfy a desire as behavior caused by that desire. People do sometimes act in an effort to satisfy desires that they had prior to acting. But I say that the phrase "I wanted to . . ." does not classify an action as one of those to be understood as an effort to satisfy an antecedent desire. The universal availability of "I wanted to . . ." should be evidence against the idea that it alludes to a prior desire, since satisfaction of a desire is one among many alternative backgrounds for action.

There is a sense in which "I wanted the light on" and "I thought that would get the light to go on" contrast with "She wanted the light on" and "She thought that would get the light to go on." I flip the switch and I am asked, "Why did you want the light on?" Cannot I say, "I didn't want it on, she did"? Or, to "Why did you think that switch would turn on the light?" cannot I answer "I didn't think so. I rather doubted it. She thought so." In other words, it seems that if desires or states of that genre do have a rôle here, they need not be the desire of the agent. And the same for beliefs. But the desires of others, though they may motivate my switch-flipping, will not seem as plausible as causes of my switch-flipping as my own desires and beliefs. In fact, even in these contexts we would be ill-advised to move at once to a desire-interpretation of wanting. In placing my action in the setting of what someone else wants, I need not be asserting that the sense in which she wants the light on has anything to do with her desires. I can speak of her wanting the light on, as opposed to my wanting it on, whenever I had turned it on because she was in favor of it, asked me to turn it on, or the like. I am asked, "Would you please turn on the light?" I flip the switch. I am entitled to say "She wanted the light on." But do I know anything at all about her desires? Maybe a third party asked her. Talk about "wanting" bodes nothing for desire.

The fact that the wants, desires, and beliefs of another can appear in explanatory discourse about my actions helps to dispel the illusion that references to desire and beliefs are especially strong candidates for causes of my actions. Being an agent, if a man has a desire that really is a desire (a state of desire that might exist and be appreciated prior to a satisfaction-seeking act), he can try to gratify his desire. This only manifests the same ability he has to gratify the desire of another. Mention of an agent's desire is explanatory, not because the desire caused anything, but simply because it leads us to see what objective the action had, namely, the satisfaction of the desire. When an agent explains his action, saying, "She wanted . . . ," he leads us to the goal of his action, namely, the satisfaction of her desire, if the "wanted" really alludes to a desire. Whether the desire was his or hers, reference to it furthers the intelligibility of an action only on the assumption that he acted so as to bring about the satisfaction of a desire. In other words, it is not the case that reference to an outcome in explaining an action presupposes a tacit reference to a desire, but it is the case that reference to a desire in explaining action presupposes tacit reference to an outcome.

Desires play a rôle in the explanation of actions that parallels reference to contractual obligations, moral principles, promises, the expectations of others, orders, request, rules, laws, and so on. All these generate reason-giving explanations because reference to them enables us to see the goal of the explained action. Being able to act means being able to bring it about that contractual obligations are met, or to bring it about that a promise is kept, or expectation of another fulfilled, or an order obeyed, a request acceded to, a rule followed. In just this way an agent can bring it about that a desire (whether his or not) is satisfied. We are wrong to try to generate a desire to go with every sort of reason: a desire to obey the law, a desire to follow a rule, or a desire to meet a contractual obligation. We are wrong if we say that "in order to turn on the light" only explains in virtue of a tacit "I wanted to turn on the light." In the sense in which "I wanted to. . ." is always available, it is merely another way of saying "In order to . . ." and not a further premise about prior states. In the sense in which "I wanted to . . ." can refer to something like a prior state of desire for something, *wanting* will not enter into all reason-giving explanations, and it will enter only when I have acted so as to satisfy a desire as opposed to acting because it is my job, because I promised, in order to please her, etc.

The thought that there is always a desire or something like a desire involved in actions, as a candidate causal factor, is not suggested in the least by the phenomenology of action. It originates in the requirements of a causal theory of action together with the hope that desires are more plausible as causes than other matters that are equally natural as reasons. Whatever the foundation of this theory of desire and causality, it does not even make much sense when we try to project it into the realities of desire and reason-giving.

Imagine a setting in which a man does have a desire to have a light on. "Oh, if only the light were on," he says, by way of expressing this desire. Then he sees a switch, and he forms the belief that flipping that switch would turn the light on. He flips the switch. What does the agent himself understand about his action here, so that he might try to convey that understanding to us by giving a reason for his action? Does he seem to know something about how he brought about his own action? Does he seem to be able to tell us how he got himself to flip the switch? Does he know what caused switch-flipping to take place?

It is hard to assign a clear sense to these questions, much less to suppose that in offering the explanation "I wanted to turn on the light" an agent is relying on an affirmative answer for these questions. In contrast, is it not obvious that what he understands is the end state that his action was chosen to bring about? Flipping a switch is something that a man is able to do, and, in consequence, he is able to bring about whatever can be brought by flipping switches accessible to him. A man who knows what is caused by flipping switches accessible to him has a range of potential goals. He knows that he can have the light on if he wants (or someone else does), not because he understands that wanting the light on will somehow cause him to move the switch, but because he knows that the switch turns on the light and that he can flip it.

Finally, there are contexts where causal factors are the point of explanatory discussions of actions, and these contexts offer sharp contrasts with reason-giving explanation. We can describe actions in terms of their effects in ways that provoke curiosity satisfiable only by explaining how causal factors were deployed so as to bring about an objective. I tell you that I put the engine block on the workbench, and you wonder how I managed to get that state of affairs to come about, because the engine block weighs 900 pounds. Then I explain how I deployed causal factors such as jacks or pulleys in raising the object.

Prior to this explanation you know the goal of my action, but you are left with a question of the form "That was the goal alright, but how did he get it to come about?"

Causal theorists of pro attitudes construe the explanatory function of wants and desires as though they answer to this kind of curiosity. The standard line about reason-giving insists that it is well and good to say that an action brought about such and such an outcome, but without reference to a want or other pro attitude we are entitled to ask, "That was the outcome, but how did he get something with that outcome to come about?" If this were a feasible interpretation for the rôle of pro attitudes, then "He wanted to turn on the light" would parallel "He put a jack under it." They would be offered as the causes of the motion of the engine and the switch-flipping, respectively. Where an understanding of causes is involved an agent can say, "If I could put a jack under that I could get it up on the bench." If pro attitude reasons were offered as causal illumination, they would also generate "I could have the switch flipped in no time if only I had a cause like wanting the light on." It seems reasonably certain that "I wanted the light on" is never offered as a causal explanation for switch-flipping. If this is so, then there is really no serious competition for the teleological interpretation of reason-giving explanation.

NOTES

1. See Donald Davidson, "Actions, Reasons, and Causes," *J.Phil.*, LX, 1963; reprinted in Davidson, *Essays on Actions and Events*, New York, 1980, p. 11. The phrase Davidson quotes is from A.I. Melden, *Free Action*, London, 1961, p. 184.

2. Andrew Woodfield, *Teleology*, Cambridge, 1976.

3. G. Sommerhof, *Analytical Biology*, London, 1950; and E. Nagel, "Teleological Explanation and Teleological Systems," in S. Ratner, ed, *Vision and Action*, New Brunswick, New Jersey, 1953.

4. Thus, for example, plants cannot be said to have goals according to Woodfield. See *Teleology*, p. 33. Chapter 10 of *Teleology* presents Woodfield's frankly mentalist theory of teleology.

5. Ibid., p. 171.

6. Ibid., p. 172.

7. Quoted as reprinted in H. Feigl and M. Brodbeck, *Readings in the Philosophy of Science*, New York, 1953, p. 540. Emphasis added.

8. Davidson, *Essays*, pp. 3-4.

9. Ibid., p. 3.

10. Ibid., p. 6.

11. Ibid., p. 7.

12. Ibid., p. 11.

VII

Causal Explanation and the Philosophy of Mind

1. Causality, positivism, and materialism: some recent history

No pattern of explanation is more familiar than explanations of human actions that advert to the desires and beliefs of the agent. If Sally moves a switch on the wall, we can have

Why did Sally move the switch? Sally wanted to have the light on, and she believed that switch controls the light.

Such explanations are not merely commonly given and accepted. It is also unquestionable that a great preponderance of these explanations are correct. Furthermore, although beliefs and desires get particularly prominent attention in the thinking of philosophers about the explanation of actions, other mental states such as hopes, fears, and intentions have parallel rôles in explanations. Talk of a "desire-belief" model for the explanation of actions is not meant to limit explanatory relevance to these two propositional attitudes.

The prevalence of this explanatory pattern and the general recognition of the justice and correctness of many particular explanations of this type raise the question of the conceptual foundation of the insight into things that such explanations rely upon. In the 1950s and 1960s, when a philosophical specialty known as "the philosophical analysis of action" first came to be recognized, the nature of these explanations and the basis of their validity were much debated. The discussions of that period were conducted against a background of positivist analysis of the concept of explanation that required deduction of what is explained from premises that include general statements or laws for any fully successful explanation.[1] This conception of explanation, in turn, is an expression of traditional empiricist understanding of causality and causal explanation.

Since the time of Hume empiricists have agreed that no causal nexus will be discovered and that, ultimately, the insights that are expressed as causal explanations derive all of their explanatory and predictive power from our success in seeing events as instances of general laws. The positivist doctrine was presented under the rubric "the logic of explanation," but it is really an assertion of confidence in the Humean point of view about causality reexpressed in the jargon of logic to fit the needs of a school of philosophy that made the scornful rejection of all metaphysics its cardinal tenet. Positivists gave the subject matter thus conceived the honorific title "scientific explanation." All ideas about explanation that could not be accommodated by Humean thinking on causality, as restated in the "formal mode"[2] of speech, were rather dogmatically rejected.

The ruling positivist doctrines about explanation induced social scientists and historians to suppose that their real work consists in seeking out laws within their subject matters from which they might try to deduce whatever they hoped to explain. Performances short of this deductive ideal were only "explanation sketches," in the phrase of Carl Hempel, who was the most prominent spokesman for the positivist account of explanation.[3] The actual direction of empirical research was affected by the ruling positivist doctrine about explanation and causality. For decades psychology was virtually confined to behaviorist learning theory partly because this topic seemed to offer the best chance for development of theories with empirical laws under which something might be subsumed. These unproductive methodological strictures offset the beneficial influence of positivist tough-mindedness and demand for clarity. The positivists were unable to treat causality under that name because theories about causality were banished as "metaphysics." Logic and especially the logical structure of science were permitted enterprises on the paired-down roster of presentable philosophical subject matters. What had been studied under the heading "causality," insofar as a legitimate residue of it remained, had to be the logic of something, and "the logic of explanation" seemed innocent enough. But the shift in philosophical vocabulary itself generated false doctrine. The positivists did not reflect on, much less analyze, the concept of explanation. Instead they presented a standard empiricist view about causality under an inappropriate name. As a result an unargued-for presumption that all explanation is causal explanation gained currency.

Reflection on the sorts of things to which explanations are addressed suffices to refute the notion that the positivists arrived at their views by analyzing the concept of explanation. We ask for, give, and are enlightened by explanations of notations, proofs, theories, protocol, conduct, symbols, poems, gestures, games, sayings, conventions, myths, meanings, rituals, jokes, methods, theories, systems, structures, regularities, irregularities, contracts, laws, procedures, arrangements, routes, failures, omissions, and riddles. We also explain events, and positivists frequently fell into the habit of using the phrase "the event to be explained" as if all explanations explain events. Of course, it is true that only events are subsumed under laws, and it is only of events about which it is entirely natural to think that we are illumined when we find out their causes.

From the positivist perspective efforts at noncausal interpretation of reason-giving explanation seemed to be an inadequate tender-minded challenge to the Humean outlook. A number of philosophers belonging loosely to the Oxford analytic school and also loosely influenced by Wittgenstein put the case against a causal interpretation of reason-giving in an elegant, sensitive, and persuasive rhetoric.[4] However, with the growing popularity of materialism (which automatically solves the problem of mind-body interaction) support for noncausal interpretation diminished, and then noncausal interpretations virtually disappeared when the noncausal position of the Oxford Wittgensteinians was perceived to lack cogency upon close examination.[5]

I emphasize the mutual encouragement of the positivist "logic of explanation" and the identity-theory format in the philosophy of mind. If all explanation is causal, then beliefs and desires which figure prominently in correct explanations of actions are among the causes of those actions. As such, beliefs and desires *must be* events or states of subjects belonging to the temporal period prior to and up to the actions they explain and cause. A strong commitment to the positivist doctrine of explanation inevitably carries with it the confidence that beliefs and desires simply have to be inner realities in those who believe and desire. Otherwise the causal rôle of these mental things would be utterly unintelligible. Once the logic of explanation has forced us to construe beliefs and desires as inner realities in agents, we will have to incline to a physical identification of the inner realities so as to think of them as exerting causal efficacy in the physical world.

The most influential critical examiner of noncausal interpretations of reason-giving in the 1960s was no doubt Donald Davidson, whose refutation of the main thrust of the anticausal position exerted a decisive influence on subsequent thinking about reason-giving. The prominence that the mind-brain identity theory had achieved, a prominence which rapidly became virtual consensus, contributed to the climate of opinion in which the prospects for a noncausal analysis of reason-giving explanation evaporated altogether.

The emergence and widespread adoption of "functionalist" philosophy of mind can be viewed as a sophistication of, rather than a replacement for, materialism. Most functionalists envision a material realization for the functional states with which mental phenomena are to be identified. The metaphysical underpinning of functional states is not an issue on which functionalist philosophy of mind itself dictates a position, and it is said, in consequence, that functionalism is compatible with dualism. However, the outlook of functionalism is so conspicuously rooted in causal understandings and anti-Cartesian behaviorism, and functionalism is so indebted to materialist thinking, generalized to avoid introducing the empirical facts of human physiology into the logical analysis of mental concepts, that the claim that functionalism is not essentially materialistic is of small interest. Apart from those philosophers who would not mind rehabilitating the problems of mind-body interaction (as far as I know there are none) the causal focus of functionalism by itself indicates a materialist commitment.

Davidson and later advocates of the causal interpretation of explanations that cite beliefs and desires were satisfied that the arguments of the noncausal theorists were inadequate, and they paid little attention to the intuitive considerations that led some Oxford analysts and Wittgensteinians to propose a noncausal analysis of reason-giving. Davidson, like the positivists, advances an essentially Humean conception of causality together with the conviction that beliefs and desires must be causes if they are to have any explanatory relevance at all to actions.[6] There are, however, intuitive grounds for supposing that beliefs and desires are not causes of the actions they explain. These intuitions do not immediately suggest any alternative model for explanation, and this is the fact on which Davidsonian rejection of noncausal analysis has concentrated.

If causal relations are not the ultimate support of explanatory claims, and if no other conception of the claims is provided, we cannot simply endorse a general permissiveness that accepts explanations that seem intuitively right without any articulated rationale for the objective validity of such intuitions. This is a reasonable viewpoint. The current inattention to the very possibility of a noncausal understanding of reason-giving is, however, a late effect of positivist repression.

2. Intuitions contrary to causal interpretation

But what are these intuitions to which those who accept the causal picture are presently so inattentive? In this section I will discuss two pretheoretical lines of thinking about explanations that invoke beliefs and desires, both of which make these explanations of actions seem quite remote from causal explanations that fit Humean constraints. First, I will show that given the relevant belief and desire (with other needed factors), the explained action cannot be thought to simply occur. On the contrary, it must still be *undertaken* or *performed* by the agent if it is to occur at all. This alone makes it very difficult to see reference to desires and beliefs in a causal light. Second, I will show that the Humean causal interpretation leaves no room at all for the concept of the ability to act. Explanation in terms of beliefs and desires presupposes the ability of the agent to perform the action in question with or without the specific reasons that induce the agent to act and, thereby, to exercise the presupposed ability. This pattern of thinking, too, conflicts with causal analysis.

(i) When a desire-belief explanation is apt and correct, everyone knows that all sorts of other conditions are required in whose absence the action would not follow. For example, obstacles may stand in the agent's way, and given the actual mix of obstacles and opportunities, further beliefs, desires, fears, and expectations, of unlimited variety, may inhibit, redirect, or cancel the impulse to action. Appreciation of this complexity is not something that is missed by the causal interpretation of belief and desire explanations. If we follow the causal pattern of analysis, however, we are obliged to think that when all the right auxilliary conditions, including other mental states, are present (and inhibiting conditions are absent), then the action does simply follow.

By way of comparison, when we think that the injection of an antibiotic causes the elimination of an invading bacterial colony in a human body, we know that the antibiotic does not always suffice. The antibiotic sometimes fails to get rid of the infection. But to suppose that the injection of an antibiotic causally explains the elimination of a particular bacterial infection in a particular person on a specific occasion is to think that it did suffice, given other conditions, on that occasion. That is, with some further conditions and circumstances which we might have trouble fully specifying in detail, the elimination of the infection does *simply happen* if the antibiotic (in the appropriate quantity etc.) is introduced. If in the particular case explained a cause is rightly identified, we are able to see the case as an instance of a general law (even though we may not be able to state the law fully).

We can maintain the explanation "The injection caused the elimination of the infection" in the face of cases where injection is not followed by the elimination of the bacteria, but we can do this only insofar as we think that some circumstance or condition needed along with the injection was not present in the irregular cases where injection does not lead to elimination of infection. If they are not covered by this kind of other-things-being-equal clause, counterinstances to the law defeat the causal claim.

To bring out the significance of this elementary Humean line of thinking about causality for the causal interpretation of reason-giving explanation, we should try to imagine our grounds for rejecting a causal claim in the context of this medical example. Imagine, for instance, that it is claimed that some mail-order "scientifically proven" tonic eliminates infections. Upon testing suppose it turns out that whatever the other conditions and factors present or absent, infection continues unabated. We would certainly reject the claimed efficacy of the tonic. We would not be patient with the manufacturer's defense:

> Well, although our product causes the eradication of infections, you cannot use it by itself; you have to take the tonic, and then having taken it, you have to get rid of the infection yourself. Infections do not just automatically get eliminated. You yourself have to get rid of the infection after and in addition to taking our tonic.

This would be a concession of worthlessness. Among intuitive reasons for *not* thinking that beliefs and desires are causes is that discourse quite analogous to this spurious defense of the tonic above is not spurious in the setting of action, but, on the contrary, natural and correct.

Given all the relevant desires and beliefs Sally has, together with whatever additional factors and circumstances need to be mentioned, it is simply not the case at all that the action of switch-throwing simply follows or just happens. On the contrary, nothing at all simply happens. With all of these factors in place, Sally still has to turn on the light herself. She has to throw the switch and cannot repose confidence in the idea that the causes for its getting thrown are present, as she certainly might reasonably repose confidence in the antibiotics that do causally exterminate bacterial infections. But this circumstance does not generate doubts about the claimed explanation. We could say to Sally:

> Switches do not move automatically simply because you want something that you believe would be attained by throwing the switch. In addition to wanting the light to be on, and believing that throwing the switch would get it to be on, you have to throw the switch.

This discourse by no means weakens the explanatory relevance of the belief and desire when Sally does throw the switch, while the parallel discourse in the context of a causal analysis rebuts the explanatory relevance of the purported cause.

(ii) From the Humean point of view causes are not absolutely necessary for events of the type which they in fact produce in particular circumstances. So, a blow with a hammer may cause a glass to break, but the glass could have been broken in other ways. Nonetheless, in the sequence of events that actually unfolded it is right to say that the hammer blow caused the break. It was, we could say, necessary relative to the set of sufficient conditions under which the glass did break. If circumstances differed only in that the glass was not hit with a hammer and no alternative sufficient conditions were introduced, then we understand that the glass could not have broken. This side of causal thinking is the locus of another intuitive difficulty confronting the idea that explanations adverting to beliefs and desires are causal explanations.

It is out of place and surely false to suppose that in the circumstances of the particular action the presence of the belief and desire that explain Sally's switch-throwing was a necessary condition for switch-throwing by Sally, in the sense that in the absence of alternative sufficient conditions she could not have thrown the switch without the belief and desire that explain why she did throw it.

To be sure, we may feel entitled to say that Sally would not have thrown the switch had she not had this reason or some other reason for doing so. But we do not think that she *could* not have thrown the switch in the absence of a desire or belief, as we do feel that a caused action could not happen in the absence of a causal factor that was operative, assuming there was no other causally sufficient condition present. On the contrary, the explanation presupposes that throwing the switch is something that Sally can do, *simpliciter*. Throwing the switch is within her power. We might even express this by saying, "Of course, Sally can throw the switch, if she wants," but this does not mean "if the right cause for switch-throwing is present." John Austin pointed out thirty years ago that the "if" here is like that of "There are biscuits on the sideboard if you want them."[7] The unconditioned "There are biscuits on the sideboard" is entailed by this assertion. In the same way throwing the switch is something Sally can do, and the addendum "if she wants" is intended to emphasize that throwing the switch is in her power. The "if" clause does not mention a condition whose satisfaction is needed for the possession or the exercise of power to throw the switch.

It makes sense to speak of conditions under which Sally *is able* to throw a switch. For example, she must not be paralyzed, chained to the radiator, under the power of a hypnotist who forbids it, or utterly enfeebled by malaria. If Sally has not the strength, or opportunity, or if she is subject to some effective restraint, then she cannot throw the switch. But if she lacks only the desire for something switch-throwing can produce, or only the belief that the switch controls something she wants, then at most it may be that she will not throw the switch, although she can.

The following conditional propositions and their unconditional transformations are uniformly intelligible:

"Sally can throw the switch now
    if she has regained her strength,"
    if she has been unchained,"
    if she has recovered from the paralysis,"
    if she is no longer in a trance."

To each of these there corresponds an unconditional assertion:

"Sally can throw the switch now
    for she has regained her strength,"
    for she has been unchained,"
    for she has recovered from the paralysis,"
    for she is no longer in a trance."

But a completely different kind of thought is expressed in "Sally can throw the switch now, if she wants to," which is simply unintelligible in the unconditional form "Sally can throw the switch now, for she wants to." No one, not even a causal theorist, really wants to say that the presence of a desire like wanting to throw the switch gives a person the ability to do what he desires to do. The causal theorist deletes the whole idea of ability. If desires are causes, they are simply followed by their effects, and ability does not come into it at all. But in fact some things are under our control, and of them it is right to say that we are able to do them if we want to, but unintelligible to say that we are able to do them since we want to. The things that we can do, if we want, are at our disposal in action. Desires are only relevant in explanation of behavior where we do something that is in our power to do or not. In acting we are able to manipulate causes so as to bring about what we want.

The very existence of switches is testimony to this idea. Ever so many things can be made to happen by the closing of an electrical circuit, and made to stop happening by introducing a gap in such a circuit. Switches are devices self-consciously designed to enable us to bring into play causes for the occurrence or cessation of things suitably dependent upon electric currents. Because we can certainly throw switches, all the things that can be done by throwing switches to which we have access are within our power. When we discover how something may be caused, it is always possible that we might be able to bring this something under our control by connecting the presence of the cause to a switch. Only when we can control causes do our desires become relevant to actions like switch-throwing. If I have no control over whether an event occurs or not, as I cannot control the orbit followed by the moon, then what I want has no bearing on what happens.

The irony of the causal interpretation is that those desires and beliefs that are alleged to be causes of actions would have to be, at the same time, our contribution to the occurrence of things and factors over which we do not have control. For surely no philosopher of mind will present our beliefs and desires as causes we can manipulate as we can manipulate electrical currents by throwing switches. Were we tempted to construe beliefs and desires as manipulatable causes, we would generate a regress here. Desires and beliefs are reasons for manipulations of switches. If desires and beliefs were manipulatable causes, we would need reasons for our manipulations of desires and beliefs.

In a limited way, but one which grows with our understanding and technology, we are able to have things our way in the world, and to have those events occur of which it pleases us to arrange the causality. But the causal interpretation of our understandings (beliefs) and of what it does please us to arrange (desires) eliminates the phenomenon of control, making our mental activities just some elements among the totality of causes, none of which can we manipulate.

Our reasons for throwing a switch are not prerequisite for the ability to throw a switch. Nor are our own desires among the causes we may manipulate in order to bring about what we desire. If we were really thinking causally, we would not want to say, "Since the desire was present, I could throw the switch," any more than we would say, "Since the weight was applied to it, the ceiling could collapse." If the weight caused the collapse, the collapse simply happened, given the weight and the other factors. But the switch did not simply move, given Sally's desire and some other factors. Sally moved it.

We get the same anticausal atmosphere from the point of view of explaining failures to act. If a causal factor necessary for the action was not present, we understand that the expected event could not have taken place. If the power was disconnected, the lights could not go on, however Sally positions the switch. But Sally's lazy excuse "I did not feel like getting up" has neither the same force as an explanation nor the same status for our understanding of what was possible under the circumstances. If a necessary causal condition was missing, then the event could not possibly have occurred. But we have no willingness whatever to say, "Well, you certainly could not possibly have thrown the switch, given that you did not want to get up out of the chair," or even, "You certainly could not have thrown the switch, given that you did not want something badly enough that you believed required switch-throwing."

There is a clear sense in which it is only feasible to introduce desires in the explanation of action when we believe that the agent could have performed the action even without the desire, and we believe, further, that the agent might not have acted even with the desire. It is only pertinent to advert to desires in connection with the explanation of things that we think are under the agent's control. We cannot say, "I wanted to get rid of the infection I have, and that is why I ran a high fever." We cannot say this even though the prospective elimination of the infection may be part of the correct explanation for the fever. The explanation is out of place, because we do not have any control over whether we run fevers or not. But we can explain why we kept the furnace on at full capacity and maintained our house at near 100 degrees F, saying "I wanted to get rid of mildew, and I believed keeping the house very hot would do it." Reference to a desire fits here, not because it causes me to do anything about the house temperature, but because I can do as I please about the house temperature. This means not that I will do what I desire but simply that what happens is up to me.

This distinction would be without sense if beliefs and desires were simply among the causes of actions. On that account nothing at all would be under the control of the agent and then there would be no agency. There would be causes within the body and causes outside the body. What happens would happen when the causal factors were present and not otherwise. There is no appeal to the idea of control if in explaining an action we are merely saying that a factor sufficient for its occurrence, under the circumstances, was present. On the causal picture the agent cannot do anything but the explained act when the effective desire is present. Therefore, the agent has no control of anything in that circumstance. And the agent cannot perform the act in question at all if the desire, necessary in the circumstances, is not present. Therefore, the agent never has any control over whether he does this sort of thing or not. His stance vis-à-vis what his beliefs and desires produce in the way of effects is much the same as his stance vis-à-vis what effects his gravitational mass produces.

Finally, when it comes to actions that are arduous and difficult, the contrast between causes and reasons takes on another aspect. If we find that Sally has moved an enormous rock that disfigured the lawn, we might ask, "How did a slim girl get this boulder to move?" We are satisfied when we find she used the winch on her jeep. But if she has moved a boulder from one spot to another in the middle of the woods for no visible purpose by using the winch on her jeep, we are not similarly enlightened by being told, "She had the desire to do it." Of course, even a complicated project might be undertaken rather idly. But generally the validity of the explanation "I wanted to do it (and all the other necessary conditions were satisfied)" is quite limited. Explanations that invoke the vocabulary of desires are often statements of the end for which an action is undertaken and not references to prior circumstances at all. That is why the explanation "Sally moved that boulder four feet to the north because she wanted to move the boulder four feet to the north" is so unsatisfactory. Desire-belief explanations are expected to make what has been done fit into some schema within which it will seem intelligible, reasonable, or plausible in terms of recognizable needs or recognizable satisfactions. It is for this reason that the smart aleck's explanation "I did it because I felt like it" is not intended as, and does not strike us as, a true, albeit minimal, explanation citing an antecedent desire as cause, but as a refusal to cooperate in providing any explanation at all.

The relationship between purposes and explanations that cite desires and beliefs was explored in chapter 6. Those discussions constitute an interpretation of reason-giving explanations that does not assume that beliefs and desires are relevant to actions because they cause the agent's behavior. For the purposes of a preliminary outlook on the philosophy of mind I think it correct to say that philosophers would not be tempted to construe reason-giving explanations causally, and to construe the causes invoked physically and mechanically, were it not for a conviction that no other interpretation is either plausible or in accord with deeply held convictions about scientific intelligibility. The causal interpretation has to ride down the natural understanding that though a person may act to satisfy a desire, to speak of the desire in explanation of the action is not to refer to a factor that made his behavior inevitable under the circumstances. Chapter 6 provides a noncausal interpretation of reason-giving and thereby rebuts the claim that explanations of actions advert to causes if they really get any explaining done.

3. The desire-belief model for explanation of action

Here are two explanations of an action. (DB) is a desire-belief explanation. (DK) is a desire-knowledge explanation.

(DB) Q: Why did you throw the switch?
     A: Because I wanted the lights on, and I *believed* that switch controls the lights.

(DK) Q: Why did you throw the switch?
     A: Because I wanted the lights on, and I *knew* that switch controls the lights.

As it stands, (DK) cannot be construed causally. Knowing that p requires that p be true. Therefore knowledge cannot be identified with some inner state or activity in an agent, and for that reason knowledge is not interpretable as an inner cause having the switch-throwing among its effects. No contemporary philosopher of mind proposes an identity theory of knowledge. The shift to a causal understanding of the explanation requires, first, the substitution of "believe" for "know" and, second, an inner-state interpretation of belief. Thus, a materialist identity theory of mental phenomena will identify the agent's *desire* that the light be on and the agent's *belief* that the switch in question controls the light as neural states or processes in the agent's brain. Then these neural items can be presented as part of the causal history of the movement of the switch.

Cartesian dualist explanations of action can have the same causal form, but dualism takes on the intractable burden of the problem of mind-body interaction since nonmaterial inner realities are supposed to cause physical events in the agent's body, and, thence, in his environment. Of recently developed philosophies of mind, functionalism most obviously presents a causal interpretation of (DB). Beliefs and desires are *identified*, on functionalist principles, by appeal to a rôle in causal relations. Belief that p is a functional state of an organism (or a machine) defined, not in terms of any physical description, but in terms of the rôle the state plays in mediating causes and effects.[8] Thus, it is a built-in feature of functionalist philosophy of mind that desire-belief explanations are causal explanations adducing inner states of the organism as causes of what is explained.

Could we construe beliefs as inner states of agents, and accept reference to those beliefs in explanation of actions, but reject the idea that the resulting explanations are causal? This format, if such is tenable at all, demands some account of the explanatory relevance of inner-belief states and desires. If they are not causes, then what do beliefs have to do with what happens?

I do not intend to argue for a noncausal understanding of explanatory appeals to the inner states of agents here. I will argue that reason-giving explanation is not properly understood as a variety of causal explanation, but I assert this on the ground already presented in chapter 2 that beliefs are not inner states of agents at all, or inner realities of any kind that might cause anything whatever. I will ignore desires for the moment, because an analysis that excludes the inner-state interpretation of belief suffices for the refutation of the causal interpretation of desire-belief explanations of actions.

It is universally agreed that one cannot know what is false. So the truth of "The switch controls the lights" is required for the truth of "I know that the switch controls the lights." We cannot be confident in an ascription of knowledge that p if we are unsure about p itself, since p is entailed by "S knows that p." This is why (DK) cannot be interpreted as a causal explanation. Since the truth of p has nothing to do with S and his states, there is no such thing as a state of knowing that p which might exist in a subject and might cause actions. After learning everything there is to learn about S's states, we would have to check the rest of the universe to see if p is true before we could be sure that "S knows that p" is true.

In contrast, "S believes that p" can be true whether p is true or not. When we reflect on the explanations (DB) and (DK), it seems right to think that the latter does rest on the former. Most philosophers, Plato is an exception, think that belief that p deserves a place in the philosophical analysis of knowledge that p. "I believed that p" is a universally unavailable restatement for the claim "I know that p" when p turns out to be false. And if we reject a speaker's qualifications for claiming to know that p, while accepting the sincerity of his endorsement of p, we will automatically downgrade his knowledge claim and impute belief that p to him.[9]

When S throws the switch because he knows that switch controls the lights, it is not the fact that the switch does control the lights that is pertinent. Even if S, contrary to the hypothesis, is wrong about the switch, he would have thrown it, given his mental state. So it is S's mental state, that is, his belief that the switch controls the lights, that gets the relevant explaining done. Knowledge is not a mental state. Therefore, if causally understood, (DK) implies that a mental state of S related to S's knowledge that p caused his switch-throwing. Belief that p is that mental state.

I argue, however, that the connectedness to the world that excludes knowledge from the roster of mental states also excludes belief. Therefore, although it may be that the explanation (DK) relies on an implied explanation (DB), neither explanation can be construed causally. "S believes that p" requires a truth-value for p just as "S knows that p" requires that p be true.

We have shown in chapters 2 and 3 that a statement to the effect that the speaker has the belief that p, whatever the linguistic vehicle for such a statement, must involve the assertion that p is true. The truth of p cannot be deemed a further matter on which a speaker who says that he holds the belief that p might be committed or uncommitted. But any understanding of belief that identifies believing that p with the presence of an inner state, activity, or condition would immediately authorize first-person reports of that state, activity, or condition. Given the identification, such reports would be assertions saying that the speaker believes that p, but they would necessarily be neutral on p itself. This is what we showed to be unacceptable. Furthermore, we have shown that although third-person ascriptions of belief are neutral concerning the truth of the belief itself, this is only a consequence of the fact that the believer is not the speaker. In other words, this neutrality cannot be interpreted as an indication that belief that p can be identified with some p-neutral state of the believer. For that is just the identification that will engender incoherent first-person belief statements. Finally, we have seen that the fact that the statement "I believe that p" is not false in case p is false does not show that this form of words has an asserted content other than p. The phrase "I believe that" indicates some reservation or insecurity that makes the unqualified assertion of p inappropriate. It is because "I believe that" contains this allusion to the possibility of error that this statement manages to be true, although p is false. In this connection we compared "I believe that p" with "p or I am much mistaken," which is also an expression of belief that p, a way of asserting p, and a formulation that is insulated against the possibility of falsehood even if p is false. It manages this feat by disjoining the possibility of error with the assertion of p. The error which will save the truth of the whole assertion is, of course, the error of taking the first disjunct to be true. So the disjunctive formula does not indicate a p-neutral subject matter concerning which expressions of belief are assertions.

Now let us consider another disjunctive formulation for both ascriptions and expressions of belief:

> S has the true belief that p,
> or S has the false belief that p,

and in the first person:

> I have the true belief that p,
> or I have the false belief that p.

The latter expression of belief that p is also insulated from falsehood even in cases where p is false. These disjunctive statements express exclusive alternatives. A subject S has the belief that p just insofar as one or the other of the disjuncts holds of S. But whichever disjunct it is that holds, it includes a truth-value for p as part of its assertive force. The first disjunct requires the truth of p, and the second the falsehood of p.

Like "S knows that p," "S has the true belief that p" requires that p is true, and therefore this disjunct cannot hold in virtue of an inner state of S. In parallel fashion, "S has the false belief that p" cannot express the presence of an inner state because it requires the falsehood of p. So what this disjunctive form asserts cannot be explicated in terms of inner realities in believers. But the disjunction does express the essence of believing.

The disjunctive interpretation of belief has an intuitive foundation. From the perspective of the believer, to decide whether to believe that p is to decide whether p is true or false. To believe that p is to take p to be true, and to report belief that p is to assert that p is true. Of course, taking p to be true and asserting that it is does not guarantee that p is in fact true. So there is an element of risk. The believer will be wrong if p is false. But the risk of error along with the possibility of getting something right comes directly from the stand taken on p. There is no room for an inner state of the subject, mediating between the subject and the subject matter of the belief. There is no state of belief that the subject might report without asserting that p. In short, believing that p is standing in one or the other of two epistemic relations to the subject matter of which p is true or false. Being right or wrong, having the true belief or the false belief, are expressions for these two epistemic relations.

4. The impulse to salvage an inner state

A natural reaction here, which everyone thinking about these matters, including this writer, will feel, is that there must be something in or about the subject S in virtue of which, in case p is true, S has the true belief that p, and in case p is false, he has the false belief that p. In contemplating this reaction I want to insist that this something in or about S cannot be identified as *S's state of belief that p*. Perhaps those who have been persuaded by the evident troubles that such an identification generates will agree that no inner state in virtue of which S is right if p is true and wrong if p is false can be identified as "S's state of belief that p." If an inner something is needed, it will have to be called something else.

Provisionally let us use the letter B for this state of or feature of believers that p. The point is that if there were no factor B, that is, something present in or true about S, the discovery that p is true or is false could not lead to the idea of S's being right or wrong. The mere fact that p is true does not entail that S is right about something or that S has the true belief that p. There has to be something about S that, together with the truth of p, entails that S has the true belief that p. Even if we cannot call this inner item "S's belief that p" because that would authorize incoherent self-ascriptions, the state must exist, and many or most of the things that identity theorists have wanted to say about belief states will hold of the state B.

For all its naturalness this line of thinking that introduces something in the rôle of B cannot be allowed. The temptation I share to accept B with the proviso that whatever B is, it is not S's belief that p, is a temptation to readmit all the difficulties and confusions that we have been trying to eliminate from our understanding of belief.

The pattern of thinking to which we are all susceptible here emerges first in the setting of our understanding of knowledge. It is worth reminding ourselves that the fact that knowledge cannot be identified with an inner state of the knower has become clear to the consensus of epistemologists and philosophers of mind only within the last few decades. This belated understanding is a measure of the tenacity with which the inner-reality picture grips our sense of the options available in the philosophy of mind. For, once the error is pointed out, it seems quite surprising that philosophers should have persevered as long as they did in the thought that knowledge might be an inner state of a knower. In introducing a factor B in thinking about belief that p we are suffering from the Cartesian yearning for an inner reality that makes the impossibility of a rôle for such a factor curiously invisible to philosophers.

When the idea of a mental state of knowledge was finally set aside, the replacing view salvaged as much of the story of an inner reality as possible. So philosophers said to themselves,

> Of course, knowledge that p cannot be an inner state since it entails that p is true, and no state of a subject can guarantee that. But the old view was not entirely wrong. If S knows that p, there must be an inner state of S in virtue of which we can say of S that he knows that p when we do find that p is true.

The inner state of *believing that p* was merely this salvaged item in the corrected conception of knowledge that p. Thus we find "S believes that p" as a clause for standard analyses of "S knows that p." Knowledge that p requires an inner state, although it is improper to call that inner state "the state of knowing that p."

The line of thinking that introduces an inner state B in our understanding of belief follows just the same route. I have argued that belief that p cannot be an inner state because such an account would engender incoherent first-person belief statements that fail to express any stand on the belief itself. If this line of thinking is valid, our thinking about belief and the inner will have to be revised as our thinking about knowledge and the inner was revised. Once again, our impulse is to salvage an essential element from the theory that we are obliged to amend. So we try to substitute another inner state B, which will still play an indispensable part in believing that p, although B is not to be called "the state of belief that p." We say to ourselves,

> There must be some way in which S is different when he believes that p from what he would have been had he not believed that p. This difference *in S* has nothing to do with p being true or false. If we could not specify something,

B, that is just a fact, state, condition, or circumstance about the believer S, then finding that p is true or false would not even be relevant to determining that S is right or wrong about something.

When we are in the grip of this plausible-sounding proposal, we will think that the inner item B must be something like an inner representation, perhaps a neural representation, maybe even an inscription of p in *neuralese*. In any case, it will be something that raises the general scientific and philosophical problem of the identification of B. All the old theories will be back in business, even if we are right to say that they cannot be called theories about the nature of belief states.

5. Betting and believing

The tenacious idea of an inner something in believers emerges forcefully when we compare belief and knowledge and try to amend our thinking about belief as our thinking about knowledge has already been amended. To relax the grip of this idea, I want now to compare the concepts of betting and believing. In many ways the concepts are not very close to one another. No philosopher would be tempted to propose an inner-state interpretation of betting. In spite of differences betting is a concept which is broadly of the pattern into which we try to force the concept of belief when dominated by the old Cartesian style in the philosophy of mind.

For simplicity, imagine that horse races are the only things on which there is any betting, and also that the only mechanism for making a bet is buying a parimutuel ticket at the racetrack. In order to facilitate comparison, let us speak of betting that p rather than betting on H. If p is "H wins the first race," a subject S bets that p if, and only if, S buys a win ticket for H. A number of points that I have made about belief might be replicable in the context of betting. It looks as though we could present a disjunctive analysis of betting akin to the disjunctive analysis we have proposed for belief. Every bet that p is a winning bet or a losing bet. These are exclusive alternatives. The first requires that p be true; the second that p be false. We might try to argue that betting cannot be an inner state of a subject (of course, no one says it is), since it is essentially disjunctive, and each disjunct requires a truth-value for p, which goes beyond anything that a state of S could guarantee.

A sufficient response would be this: Betting that p is not a disjunctive concept where each disjunct requires a truth-value for p. On the contrary, there is a categorically ascribable circumstance concerning S that is sufficient for the claim that S bets that p. There is something, B', which is true of S. And B' is just the same fact about S whether his is a winning or a losing bet. B', under our simplifying hypotheses, is the buying of an appropriate ticket. This is what is true of S *in virtue of which*, in case p is true, S wins, and, in case p is false, S loses. Within the scope of the pretense that betting only covers horse races and only involves ticket-buying, betting that p *is* buying a ticket for H.

In short, in the case of betting that p there is subject matter about S which can be the content of p-neutral first- or third-person statements. When S reports "I bet that p," he is saying of himself that B' is true. He is not saying that p is true, or asserting that his bet is a winning bet. S can bet that p without taking any stand on the truth of p. Generally, those who bet that p at least hope that p is true. But even this is not absolutely required. It may be rare, but is not impossible, to bet that p, while believing or even knowing that not-p. One can bet with the intention and expectation of losing. So the first-person "I bet that p" is no more an assertion of any stand on the truth of p than is the third-person "S bets that p."

This parallelism of p-neutral first- and third-person betting statements is not replicated in the analogous first- and third-person belief statements. If believing could be identified with some factual matter about the subject, as betting can be identified with such a factual matter, then p-neutral first-person belief statements would be available. But the very idea of such a statement is absurd. A bettor can say, "I bet that p, but I have no idea at all as to whether p is true or false." But a believer cannot say, "I believe that p, but I have no idea at all about the truth or falsehood of p."* To say, "I believe that p" is to

---

*There is a danger of confusion here because the words "I bet that p" are sometimes employed as an idiomatic vehicle for expressing belief that p. So, a detective discussing a murder case with his colleagues can reflect on the fit of bits of evidence and then exclaim, "I bet the butler did it." This, of course, is an expression of belief, tentative perhaps, and an assertion, qualified perhaps, that the butler did do it. There

express the stand "It's true" of p, and this is simply contradicted by the claim to have no view on that matter.

If a skeptic thinks that S does not believe that p and, therefore, inclines to reject S's statement "I bet that p," S can silence such doubts decisively by establishing that he has bought the ticket in question. That is the end of the matter, and the truth or falsehood of p has nothing to do with it, not for S and not for others. Such would be the case for the concept of belief, too, were belief that p an inner state such as an inner inscription of p. A subject could silence all doubts about his believing that p by establishing that the inner inscription of p is present in him. That would be the end of the matter, and the truth of p would have nothing to do with it, not for S and not for others. But, of course, this is madness. A person cannot simply ignore the issue of the truth or falsehood of p altogether and establish just that he believes that p.

What does this indicate concerning the disjunctive character of the concepts under discussion here? Betting, as we saw, is not a disjunctive concept, even though every bet is either a winning or a losing bet. This is irrelevant because we have a subject matter with which betting that p is rightly identified. Buying the appropriate ticket *is betting that p*, and there is nothing disjunctive about that. Betting merely sets the stage for one or the other of two alternative outcomes: the bet wins or loses. Believing is a disjunctive concept because we cannot introduce a categorically ascribable something to be identified with belief that p. The character of betting makes possible an explanatory relationship that cannot obtain in the context of believing. It is because S buys the ticket that the truth or falsehood of p is relevant to determining whether S is a winning or a losing bettor. Because there cannot be any such identification of belief, we must set aside the parallel explanation "It is because of S's state of belief that p that

---

is an elision here. The use of "bet" relies on the what is more explicit in the vernacular "I betcha. . . ." The latter does not really assert that a bet is made, since that would require the agreement to bet on the part of the person addressed. It asserts a willingness to bet which is by implication based on the belief that p. The same idea lies in the background of the use of "I bet that p" to express belief that p. The assertion contains a rhetorical assumption of a willingness to bet on the part of the hearer or some ideal gambler. These uses show not, that "I bet that p" generally expresses or indicates belief that p, but only that believing that p is one common reason, by no means necessary, for betting that p.

S is right if p is true and wrong if p is false." This explanation might be given a sense, but it cannot be a parallel for the betting case because believing that p *is* being right if p is true or wrong if p is false. It is not a state *in virtue of which* S is right or wrong, as p is true or false.

What shall we say about the demand that S must have some p-neutral state B, which (let it be conceded) is not a state of belief, but which has to be specified in order to explain the relevance of the truth or falsehood of p? We said that the truth of p, by itself, does not establish that S has the true belief that p. Surely we need something about S that taken in conjunction with the truth of p leads to this judgment on S's epistemic success. Such a "something" will be put in the rôle of the state B, and it will provide the explanation of the relevance of the truth-value of p to S's case. In this way the job performed by B will be just like that of an inner state of belief, but without that title.

This conviction that there must be something present in or true of S comes from considering our reasons for ascribing and evaluating beliefs of others. The introduction of B seems necessary when we have adopted the third-person viewpoint on S's belief that p. We have to know something about S in order to make the discovered truth-value of p relevant to our judgment that S has a true or a false belief that p. The trouble with this reflection is that, just like the inner belief-state conception of believing, it utterly falls apart when we look at belief from the point of view of the believer. S cannot say,

> Well, the mere truth of p does not yield the result that I have the true belief that p. I must have some state B, in order to make the truth of p relevant to my epistemic success.

On the contrary, S cannot make any sense at all of the need for any such state in his own case. Of course, he takes all of his beliefs to be true beliefs. That is what it is to believe something. In fact they may not be true beliefs. But if he takes it that p is true, then the fact that p is true is certainly all that is required for the judgment that he has a true belief that p. Prior to the final determination of the truth-value of p, all that S himself can say is that he may be mistaken. He is sure that he may be mistaken, not because he appreciates the presence of something, B, in or about himself, but because he takes p to be true. In saying that he bets that p S does not assert that his is a winning bet (and therefore that p is true), but in saying that he believes that p he is claiming that p, his belief, is true. The perspective of the believer deletes the demand for the inner. How would some p-neutral inner item B function at all with respect to S's belief that p in the thinking of S? It could not. The only reason for feeling that something like B must be operative is that we are long habituated by the Cartesian thinking when we contemplate mental phenomena.

6. Conclusion: the subjectivity of belief

We have to base our philosophical understanding of belief on the point of view of the believer, and we cannot make features of thinking about the beliefs of others the determining factors in our analysis. There is a sense in which belief is a subjective phenomenon. So it is reasonable that we adjust our discourse about ascription of belief so that it will fit what it is for a subject to believe that p. The concept of belief rests on the fact that we can apprehend the world and be right or wrong about it. If we were wholly without any self-knowledge and knew nothing about our inner states at all, that would not inhibit the expression of belief and discourse about belief, for a subject deciding what beliefs to adopt and to "report" need contemplate only the subject matter of his beliefs.

The subjectivity of belief brings with it a degree of privacy. In chapter 1 we touched on this privacy, and we warned against confusing privacy with privileged access to an inner reality. Only S is in a position to state S's belief that p without reference to evidence for the resulting belief statement. This subjectivity does not mean that others cannot make independent assessments of a subject's beliefs. To be sure, they can. When they make such assessments they are attempting to express in the third person what in the normal case is expressed in the first person by a subject who finds that p is true. Third-person usage has the subjective phenomena for its subject matter. Self-knowledge and the detection of inner states by a subject play no part in third person discourse. For that reason it is a mistake to suppose that the inner states of the believer ought to figure in the content of third-person belief statements.

When S takes p to be true and reports "I believe that p," there are surely physiological activities going on that are essential to his success in being right or wrong about the world in this instance. Furthermore, these activities will, the more they are known and understood, be interpreted from an information-theoretic viewpoint involving inner representations, messages, commands, transmissions, and receptions. We ought not take this kind of characterization of physiological activities as a mandate for a reductive theory that tries to project the semantic and epistemic character of the concept of belief into the nervous system. The same message-carrying understanding of neural and other physiological activities appears throughout biological studies. There is a metaphorical element in the most natural usage here, but I am far from suggesting that it should be tracked down and expelled, in positivist fashion, in favor of some antiseptic mechanical outlook that fails to express what we do understand. The aptness of a quasi-psychological understanding of biological phenomena, prominently including brain phenomena, does not favor a materialist philosophy of mind.

In a sense enzymes released in the saliva when we eat tell the stomach food is on the way so that secretion of hydrochloric acid will commence. In a sense the patterns on the wings of a butterfly contain information that is transmitted to other butterflies. In a sense the generation of antibodies in response to specific viral infections requires a flow of information through subtle channels. The use of the vocabulary of inner representations and information processing in these cases is not improper, and perhaps such language is even more attractive and essential in the setting of brain physiology. The point is that the information-processing rôle of the nervous system in the background of our mental activities is not constitutive of them as mental activities. The same sort of inner physiological states and activities, aptly framed with the vocabulary of information processing, occur in the mechanisms that underlie maintenance of constant body temperature, in the mechanisms that facilitate the coagulation of blood, and in the mechanisms that underlie memory and belief. But these inner "computational"[10] realities do not play any part in discourse about belief at the semantic and epistemic level. That is not because believing is something ethereal that could not be realized in the gross material constituents of a person. It is because the concept of belief is outer-oriented and involves being right or wrong about the world and, as such, cannot be captured by an inner activity or state of whatever sort.

If we permanently set aside the inner-state interpretation of belief, the causal understanding of reason-giving explanations of actions must be set aside too. A rather general reorganization in the philosophy of mind will be in order.

NOTES

1. See C.G. Hempel and P. Oppenheim, "The Logic of Explanation," *Phil. of Science*, XV, 1948; and C.G. Hempel, "Deductive Nomological vs Statistical Explanation," *Minnesota Studies in the Phil. of Science*, III, 1962, and numerous other publications of Professor Hempel. Also see the critical studies of the positivist account of explanation by A.W. Collins, "Explanation and Causality," *Mind*, LXXV, 1966; and "The Use of Statistics in Explanation," *Brit. J. for the Phil. of Science*, XVII, 1966.

2. Rudolph Carnap's distinction between the "material mode" and the "formal mode" is characteristic of the outlook which made it possible to present philosophical commitments and even metaphysical speculation as if it were somehow mere analysis of concepts. The very name "formal mode" constitutes an invitation to regard the analytical investigation of form, and not content, as the foundation of assertibility in the formal mode. Carnap held that traditional problems not restatable in the formal mode were pseudo-problems. See *Philosophy and Logical Syntax*, London, 1935, and *The Logical Syntax of Language*, A. Smeaton, translator, London, 1937. Those positivists who created the philosophical topic "the logic of explanation" exploited a spurious appearance of conceptual analysis in the presentation of their views. Very little reflection is required to appreciate the fact that none of the dogmas of the positivist model for explanation come from the analysis of any concepts. The view is one hundred percent derived from convictions about causality which are themselves plausible, or even compelling. Even on the supposition that the underlying convictions about causal relations are entirely correct, the positivist line is a misleading and incorrect view of explanation.

3. See C.G. Hempel, "The Function of General Laws in History," *J. Phil.*, XXXIX, 1942.

4. For example, G.E.M. Anscombe, W. Dray, S. Hampshire, H.L.A. Hart, and A.M. Honoré, A. Kenny, A.I. Melden, and G. Ryle, all of whom either opposed causal interpretation of reason-giving explanations or developed understandings of reasons and action without reference to causality. This is a list of those mentioned by Davidson in "Actions, Reasons, and Causes" as some who make the mistake of giving up causal interpretation for the explanation of action.

5. Although my sympathies lie with these opponents of the causal interpretation of reason-giving explanations, it is important to accept the fact that their miscellaneous arguments are inadequate, and sometimes ill-conceived and beside the point. Davidson ("Actions, Reasons, and Causes") is a good critic on these matters. In the early heyday of ordinary language analysis the Oxford school often came to rely on a set of argument patterns, all insisting that one conclusion or another is presupposed for the intelligibility of the *concepts that we do have*. Such reasoning actually shares in, and at least partially stems from, the prevailing positivist doctrine concerning the criterion of empirical meaningfulness. Where the logical empiricists in the methodology of scientific knowledge used meaningfulness as a tool for the repression of scientific activities deemed unsatisfactory, the analytic movement used meaningfulness as the foundation for a permissive style of thinking in which arguments that were far from conclusive could authenticate intuitively attractive philosophical ideas.

6. Davidson says, in the context of Melden's opposition to exclusion of causal understanding from reason-giving explanation, that such a view leaves us without any account at all of the "because" in "He did it because. . . ." And, commenting on Hampshire's discussion of Aristotle's proposal to treat wanting as a cause of action, Davidson says that only such a causal view offers any account for the connection of reasons and causes at all. Both of these points are from the paper already cited as reprinted in Davidson, *Essays on Actions and Events*, New York, 1980, p. 11. The relationship between Aristotle's conception of wanting as a cause and Davidson's Humean understanding of causality is tenuous. Generally, points that Aristotle makes about "causes" could as well be rendered as points about "explanatory factors." This makes it particularly risky to accept glosses in terms of causality at face value in discussions where the propriety of assimilating all explanatory analysis to Humean causal pattern is at issue.

7. J.L. Austin, "Ifs and Cans," *Proceedings of the British Academy*, 1956, reprinted in Austin, *Philosophical Papers*, J.O. Urmson and G.J. Warnock, editors, Oxford, 1961, p. 158.

8. I intentionally leave the characterization of functionalism in this sketchy form. The concept of functional states seems to me to be full of problems and obscurity. Maybe the problems are manageable, and the obscurity primarily in my thinking. I will not try to decide this because what I have to say about functionalism can safely presuppose, though perhaps contrary to fact, that the theory is clear enough, as I think the old fashioned neural identity theory is clear enough. I am concerned only with the idea that beliefs are states of believers of some kind or other which can be understood to cause actions of believers, or, in any case, to be causal factors. If this idea itself fails, which I mean to show here, the particulars of one working-out or another

need not be addressed.

9. This much understanding of the concept of knowledge favors philosophical analyses that assert: "S knows that p," if, and only if, (i) p is true, (ii) S believes that p, and (iii) (...?...) Difficulties arise in articulating (iii) which will give the qualifications S ought to have to be a knower that p. The Gettier cases are prominent examples of these difficulties. But the clauses (i) and (ii) are not threatened by these difficulties. S cannot know that p if he does not *even* believe that p, and S cannot know that p if p is false.

10. I take this term from Fodor's use of it, and I agree with his characterization of the need for computationality in the context of inner representations. I draw the conclusion, opposite to Fodor's, that represenational theory cannot account for concepts such as belief. See especially the essays of Fodor, *Representations*, Cambridge, Massachusetts, 1981.

Index of Names

179